POLITICAL
BARGAINING

POLITICAL BARGAINING

An Introduction to Modern Politics

Thomas A. Reilly
TRINITY COLLEGE

Michael W. Sigall
WAGNER COLLEGE

W. H. Freeman and Company
San Francisco

Library of Congress Cataloging in Publication Data

Reilly, Thomas A   1943–
    Political bargaining.

    Includes bibliographies and index.
    1. Political science.   I. Sigall, Michael W., joint
author.   II. Title.
JA66.R43   320   75-38837
ISBN 0-7167-0538-9
ISBN 0-7167-0537-0 pbk.

Printed in the United States of America

9 8 7 6 5 4 3 2 1

To our wives
Abigail and Roberta

Contents

Preface

This book grew out of a dialog that began at an annual meeting of the American Political Science Association in New Orleans. As instructors of introductory political science courses, we agreed that we lacked—and needed badly—a brief and cohesive introductory statement of what politics is all about.

During hours of discussion of various alternatives, one metaphor, bargaining in the marketplace, became increasingly appealing as a model that would help explain an otherwise bewildering range of political interactions. Indeed, we reached the conclusion that each level of political behavior and interaction—from that of the individual to that of international relations—can reasonably be compared to marketplaces in which actors compete to maximize their shares of scarce resources while minimizing their expenditures.

Over subsequent weeks and months, we developed our initial concept and applied it in a straightforward fashion to the subject matter of political science. This book is the result. We hope that the reader will find it as useful in practice as we found it challenging in preparation.

We thank Richard J. Lamb, without whose confident support this book would not have been published. We also gratefully acknowledge the patient editing of Lawrence W. McCombs and the stimulating suggestions of E. Spencer Wellhofer. A special word of thanks goes to our friend Batyah Janowski, who put us on the proverbial right track to our publisher, where several talented people helped make our book a reality.

We warmly thank our students, who were the guinea pigs for our ideas and whose responses and questions helped us to refine our own thinking. We also are glad to acknowledge our intellectual debt to our mentor, Arnold A. Rogow.

To these and other friends and colleagues who made this work a happy adventure goes the credit for whatever merit may be contained in the ensuing pages. Being co-authors, each of us can attribute any mistakes to the other.

Thomas A. Reilly
Michael W. Sigall

November 1975

Introduction

No matter how diverse our backgrounds and interests, we all interact with and within the political system. In one way or another, *every* aspect of our lives—what we do for a living, what we study, where we live, what groups we join—is touched by decisions emanating from the public sector of society. As we seek to satisfy our needs and desires, we make demands on our governmental structures and public officials for a share of the resources of society. These resources are limited, and many groups and individuals are making competing demands for them. Thus, most people seldom receive all that they want. Public officials, with the ultimate responsibility for allocating society's goods and services among the members of the society, must compromise and choose among the competing demands reaching them. An important consideration in the allocation of resources is that, if most citizens get enough of what they need and want to keep them minimally satisfied, then they will presumably support the society and uphold the values and beliefs that keep it operating.

Because political science seeks to understand the ways human beings interact with one another and with groups and institu- . tions, it is a discipline that can be important to persons of every culture or life-style. We should note that, although the study of political science is rewarding, it is also a constant challenge and a potential source of frustration. In a first look at political science, it is important not to become confused by what may seem like an endless maze of conflicting premises and approaches. The discipline is relatively new among fields of inquiry, and it has grown both in scope and in sophistication during recent years. As in any rapidly changing field of study, there is considerable confusion and dispute, much of it the result of misunderstandings rather than substantive disagreements. There are also, of course, areas of scholarly dispute. However, the newcomer to the field should strive for a broad picture of areas of general agreement and should avoid getting bogged down in methodological semantics.

Whether one is studying comparative law, the psychology and impact of personality on political leadership, or the structure of the United Nations bureaucracy—just to mention a few possible areas of inquiry—one is well within the bounds of political analysis. Yet the techniques needed to approach such diverse concerns of political scientists may vary, and the methodology that best suits a research design aimed at unraveling the mysteries of public opinion may be quite different from that required for a probing psychological examination of a historical personality, or for an assessment of the decision-making dynamics in an international crisis. These hypothetical projects are not unrelated; they are united by an underlying desire to understand the behavior and interaction of people as they try to satisfy their needs and desires from allocations of scarce resources.

We do not mean to be glib about questions of methodology. Different foci of interest may well require different analytical approaches. For example, the student of politics should be careful not to misapply a tool that is useful for answering questions about individual behavior to questions about group dynamics or international relations.

With these words of caution in mind, the reader need not feel intimidated by the prospect of embarking upon the study of politics. The state of the discipline may produce some minor bewilderment, but we hope that this book communicates in a coherent fashion both the scope of political science as a discipline and a sense of the unity of what we call politics. We are not trying to propose a universal model for political behavior nor are we advocating a particular methodological approach. We are trying to provide a way to understand the subject matter of the discipline.

We use here the metaphor of exchange, stated in language and with examples that the newcomer to the discipline can readily appreciate. We believe that this approach provides a valid view of political science as an evolving, multifaceted field of inquiry into human and social behavior and interaction. For the teacher, this way of visualizing the field permits the communication of the discipline's lack of precision and its complexity in a positive manner. For the student, the approach reveals the unity of the discipline as well as the inevitable gaps in its knowledge; it offers a coherent overview of the political world—from the behavior of individual voters to the behavior of nations in the international system. For those who expect to enter the discipline, it is important to note that the exchange model has been found fruitful by many political scientists as a guide to their research.

In this book, we have divided political science into three parts. There are other ways to divide the discipline, and each way is admittedly arbitrary to some extent. The presentation used here incorporates the major subjects covered by the discipline and allows the student to see the totality of the field.

Part I. The Political Marketplace

Part I deals with politics as a field of inquiry and raises questions, some pertaining to understanding theories of politics, and others relating to the behavior and interactions of individuals and societies. In this part, we shall try to isolate major themes of political science and to state them in terms of political exchange. We shall begin in the first chapter by examining the nature of political science as a meaningful and orderly area of analysis; we shall then probe the nature and purpose of institutions of government and of the political process within society. We shall discuss the process of political socialization, its operative mechanisms, and its relationship to the society. In essence, Chapter 1 should provide the student of politics with a basic familiarity with the discipline and should offer a basic understanding of the nature of politics, government, and the broad interweaving between the individual and the political society.

Chapter 1 also introduces the metaphor of exchange as the essential model to be used throughout this book in discussing politics. Using this model, we can approach the analysis of politics at any level by seeking to understand how individuals and groups act in order to achieve the greatest gain for the least cost—to strike a bargain that will maximize their own profits.

This basic model seeks to explain political behavior in terms of rational choices made to further self-interest. We assume that each bargainer in the political marketplace seeks to maximize his own profit or satisfaction. At first glance, this may seem like a cynical viewpoint that denies any possibility of altruistic behavior. However, we are not assuming that money and other immediate tangible benefits are the only factors to be considered in political exchanges. The satisfaction that comes from an act believed to be just or patriotic can be an important factor in a person's decision to make a particular choice. In striking his bargain, he may well reject alternatives that seem to offer greater material gains in order to obtain self-satisfaction or approval from others for an altruistic or far-sighted act. However, we must keep in mind that our model is a theoretical explanation; we observe that individuals or groups make certain choices, and we then seek to explain those choices on the assumption that the bargainers are trying to maximize their own gains. The validity of this assumption must be tested by application to many real examples; if it is valid, it should lead to an economical and coherent explanation of political reality. If we should find ourselves forced to postulate an ever-growing catalog of unlikely forms of satisfaction, each jury-rigged to fit a particular example, we would have to question our basic assumption very strongly. However, we believe that this book illustrates the simplicity and coherence of the exchange metaphor over a wide variety of political phenomena.

Chapter 2 carries these concerns into the more specific area of legitimacy. The concepts introduced in Chapter 1 are applied to a consideration of the stability of political systems and the variables that convert mere power into an authoritative exercise of power. This discussion leads to an assessment of social movements and change, gradual and systemic as well as rapid or antisystemic. The role of ideology in the dynamic processes of legitimacy and change is examined, but we do not undertake specific analysis of the ideas of liberty and equality, because there is too great a potential for normative confusion in dealing with these concepts. Yet we are aware that any discussion of the relationship between citizen and state cannot properly avoid these crucial political and moral ideas.

The concepts of liberty and equality are treated implicitly throughout this book, but it may be helpful to look briefly in this introduction at the way that they can be defined in terms of the exchange model. Liberty may be seen as the relative number of choices made available to the individual: the wider the scope of alternative courses of action for an individual on the political scene, the greater the amount of meaningful liberty. Conversely, the smaller the array of options among which an individual or group can choose, the less liberty exists. If most of the potential choices for an individual are associated by the state with severe penalties or deprivations, they cease to be meaningful choices and liberty is restricted. In effect, liberty is a measure of the extent to which the society permits individuals to act in different ways and still to succeed within the society. Put another way, it measures the degree to which an individual is free from societal sanctions that limit the modes of behavior available to him.

Equality, in a given political society, can be measured by the relative number of potential bargainers who have access to the political marketplace of the society—that is, by the proportion of the population that has an opportunity to bargain for a minimally satisfying share of the scarce resources being distributed by the society. Lack of equality, then, implies a restriction of access to the marketplace for a significant proportion of the population.

Although the concepts of liberty and equality may appear similar, they are actually in competition in the dynamic give-and-take bargaining that constitutes so much of political interchange, for there is a continuous tradeoff between liberty and equality. The more access there is for diverse groups and large numbers of people to the political marketplace, the less likely it becomes that the society will be able to tolerate numerous options and numerous alternative choices for each individual or group in the marketplace. When equality of access is broadened, it usually is necessary to narrow the liberty of the bargainers in the marketplace. Conversely, a great degree of personal liberty for bargainers in the marketplace usually can be achieved only by severely limiting access to the marketplace. The reasons for this tradeoff should become clear through the examples discussed in Part I.

Part II. National Exchange

Part II addresses the question of national politics, using both American and foreign examples and comparisons, so that we may visualize as political markets the governmental institutions created for the purpose of facilitating exchanges and allocating resources. Chapter 3 deals with structures of the American political society that engage in policy making and structures and processes that account for the making of demands on the system by competing interests. Chapter 4 examines these same political markets and exchanges in Western Europe and the Soviet Union, and relates these considerations to the concept of modernization in the Third World. Chapter 4 concludes with an attempt to apply this way of visualizing politics to the People's Republic of China.

Part III. International Exchange

Part III deals with the international political scene by treating it as a market in which nations act as bargainers in political exchanges. Chapter 5 discusses both historical and contemporary forms of international exchange. Chapter 6 looks at specific structures created on the international level to facilitate exchanges among diverse political cultures. Chapter 7 analyzes the use of law and of violence by competing worldwide interests in efforts to establish or to alter the rules of international political exchange.

We feel that the metaphor of exchange will prove illuminating for the student and will generate interest by what it reveals both about the nature of politics and about the areas where we still lack knowledge. In visualizing politics as a continuous exchange, one may see the unity of the discipline at all levels, while simultaneously appreciating the finer analytical distinctions among the levels. How political actors behave in the process of exchange, how the rules and structures are made and altered, how gains and losses are perceived and calculated, how this entire dynamic system is rationalized—these are the questions that make political science a great challenge.

The Political
Marketplace

PART I

Politics as a Field of Inquiry

CHAPTER 1

OBJECTIVES, THEORY, AND METHOD

Perhaps we should begin by confessing that political science is a bit like that animal called a "guinea pig," which is neither a pig nor from Guinea. As a group, political scientists share no firm agreement about where the political domain begins and ends, nor do they agree about their obligations as scientists.

Having said this, however, we hasten to add our view that the formal study of politics is a valuable and an immensely important endeavor. Whatever its exact boundaries, all agree that the realm of politics generally includes the affairs, policies, and objectives of government and the interactions of the groups and parties within government. Obviously, every person is affected by the politics of the society in which he lives.* In many cases, some political decision determines whether a given behavior will lead a person to a barrier or to an opportunity, will produce a reward or a punishment, or will bring a privilege or a burden. Thus, the understanding of politics can illuminate important realities that help shape our lives.

How does a society decide which behaviors are to be encouraged and which are not? In other words, how are definitive political decisions made within a society? This is the central question of political science, and it is by no means a new question. In our culture, the study of politics can be traced directly to the ancient Greek philosophers, who extensively discussed the actual or ideal interactions of citizens in a *polis*, or city-state. More recently, anthropologists and sociologists have helped us achieve a more general view of the workings of politics in a wide range of cultures.

In any society, political decisions create a network of expectations in the relationships that exist among individuals. People learn what they must do or not do if they are to succeed as members of the society; they also learn what they should expect from others. They learn the points at which the official decision-making structure will intercede on their behalf (or against them) to enforce its standards of behavior. In short, they learn what they must do and what they can get away with. If a citizen learns his lessons well, the official structure will leave him in relative peace. It may even reward him by helping him attain goals that are important to him—or those that have been judged important by the society.

This discussion would be academic if there were a boundless supply of the goods and services that people need or want. Because the supply is limited, people compete for the available resources. Often, a gain for one person or group means a loss for another. This may happen through direct competition for a particular resource, or it may happen indirectly when an official decision works out to the benefit of some, but damages the interests of others.

For example, suppose that one group wants to build a factory on a tract of unused swampy land. Another group wants to preserve the area as a bird sanctuary. If no other suitable site is available for either group, the competition between them for this limited resource must result in a gain for one group at the expense of the other. A

---

*When referring to a person of unspecified gender, we shall follow tradition and use the words "he" and "his" for the sake of simplicity.

similar result would be reached more indirectly if the society has already established zoning laws to settle such conflicts.

An important aspect of this competition is the fact that resources are distributed unequally among the people in any society. There is a stratification of advantages and disadvantages in the political competition. Some individuals and groups are in better positions to influence decisions, to reap benefits, to avoid sanctions, and to gain from the political trading a bigger share of the available resources. Having more resources to begin with and a greater capacity to convert them into political assets, the privileged stratum enters every political contest with an advantage over the lower strata. To sum up the essence of political science in the words of one of its foremost scholars, it's all a question of "who gets what, when, and how."*

The political decision-making process, then, begins with the needs and desires of people and ends with the allocation of limited resources among them. Political scientists seek an understanding of this process, but they do not all agree upon the appropriate "scientific" approach to the study. Very broadly, we can group political scientists in two general schools of method.

The first school models its approach after the analytic techniques that proved so successful in the physical sciences. Members of this school try to "break down" the complex political process into simpler components, looking for precise rules or generalizations that can summarize or predict many specific examples. Their work is characterized by quantification of data, the use of statistical principles to test the validity of research findings, and the use of mathematical models.

The other school uses an approach more common to the "humanistic" disciplines such as history. Members of this school tackle the same problems from more subjective perspectives. They make generalizations from thorough studies of a relatively small number of cases, or they apply psychological techniques to the study of a few in-depth interviews or to the analysis of documents.

Members of these two general schools employ different methods, phrase their research questions differently, and focus their investigations on different aspects of the political realm. Yet the underlying concern of any political analysis remains the same: how are

---

*Harold D. Lasswell, *Politics: Who Gets What, When, How?* (Cleveland: World Publishing Co., 1958).

the political decisions made that influence our lives? As another major modern political scientist put it, "the root is man . . . the goal is man."*

Political scientists differ, not only in their techniques of study, but also in their underlying philosophical views about man and society. Many of the classic works of political analysis in our culture were written by eighteenth-century Europeans and Americans who assumed that an individual makes rational choices for his own benefit at every level of the political process. Subsequent theories of psychology, anthropology, and sociology have tended to emphasize the nonrational influences on individual behavior. Each political scientist has some philosophical bias about the balance of rational and nonrational elements affecting individual behavior. This bias strongly affects— either explicitly or implicitly—his theories of political analysis and the kinds of research questions he poses to guide his studies.

Nonetheless, we return to the basic proposition that most political behavior involves some form of choice, whether that choice is made rationally or nonrationally. In fact, the act of choosing between alternatives is characteristic of all human behavior. Students of animal behavior tell us that an individual of any species is limited in his possible behavior patterns by a set of genetically determined "instincts" or preprogrammed responses to certain situations. Humans seem to have fewer of these built-in restrictions than do other animals. When a human reacts in a stereotyped way, it is usually because he has learned that response from his parents or from other individuals in his society. As he grows and develops, the nature and extent of his choices may change. If he moves from one social group to another, the change in behavior may be very drastic. In general, the study of human behavior involves the study of individual choices and the factors that influence them. Political science, then, is simply one subdivision of the study of human behavior. Its boundaries are necessarily vague because its subject matter overlaps with that of economics, history, sociology, psychology, and other "human sciences."

Like other students of human behavior, the political scientist often finds important insights through the study of the so-called deviant case. Generalizations about common patterns of political behavior are

_____

*Heinz Eulau, *The Behavioral Persuasion in Politics* (New York: Random House, 1963).

very useful. But understanding the exception—the deviation from "normal" patterns—often provides a key to the nature of individual choices within the totality of political society and systems.

WHY GOVERNMENT? WHY POLITICS?

We have just said that politics involves choices, and that choice is typical of all human behavior. What then distinguishes political choice from other kinds of choice? How shall we divide the universal dynamic of human beings selecting among competing alternatives into appropriate realms of political, economic, social, and personal behavior? By definition, political behavior is that behavior related to government. Government, in turn, can be defined as the set of official structures created by a society to handle its collective decision making and the allocation of limited resources among individuals and groups. A definition of politics, therefore, might best begin with a closer look at the nature and purpose of government.

Governmental institutions provide a framework for the give and take of political decisions. Governmental choices can be distinguished from personal choices, not so much by differences in the process of choice, but rather by differences in the effect of the choice. The citizens give governmental institutions the right to make policy choices that are binding upon everyone. The members of the society recognize the authority of the government to apply sanctions against any individual or group that violates governmental rules or regulations. Governmental structures, then, are distinguished by having popular authority to impose their choices upon all members of the society. Any government must have the power to apply punishments (and rewards) in order to make its citizens behave in the desired ways, whether or not they wish to. Nongovernmental groups or individuals may have some power to enforce their choices. For example, the owner of a factory may demand certain behaviors from his employees, using the threat of firing them if they refuse to obey. An official or group of officials within a religious organization might threaten excommunication if a member of the religion does not obey its rules. A social group can use the threat of ostracism to enforce its choices. However, in each of these cases, the individual has the choice of moving to another group within the society that does not recognize the authority of the owner, religion, or social group. On the other hand, the authority of a governmental institution is recognized throughout the society—except by "outlaw" groups that are regarded as enemies by the rest of society.

The power of the government to make its rules is even more significant than its power to enforce those rules. The government determines the structure of the marketplace where individuals and groups must bargain and arrive at their own choices. Governmental choices place limits upon the other kinds of choices made within the society. Governmental regulations may permit only one choice in a certain situation, may forbid certain choices while leaving a range of other possible choices, may establish rules under which individuals or groups can bargain about their choices, and may add certain advantages or disadvantages that will strongly influence the choices made by members of the society.

Whenever two or more individuals or groups compete for some limited resource, a process of bargaining must take place, if each is to obtain some part of what he wants. In this continuous process of exchanges, each agent tries to obtain as much as he can for whatever he has to give up in return. In other words, he endeavors to maximize his gains and minimize his losses in the bargaining process. Those who bargain with him, of course, are trying to do the same.

Ideally, one bargainer should be able to give the other exactly what is wanted, while obtaining his own desires in return. In practice, this ideal result can seldom be achieved. In most cases, at least one bargainer (and often both) must settle for less than he had wanted to obtain. In some cases, both bargainers may achieve their desires, but they may do so at the expense of some other member of the society. It is extremely rare for both bargainers to reach their goals while not affecting anyone else adversely.

The greater the scarcity of resources and the more complex the exchange arrangement, the more applicable is this concept of give-and-take bargaining. A marketplace must be created in which this intricate and continuous bargaining can take place. One important function of government is to establish such a marketplace where the many exchanges can transpire efficiently. In addition, the government lays down the ground rules for bargaining, so that all participants can communicate meaningfully.

Let us return to the example of the swampy land mentioned earlier. One group applies to the government for permission to construct a factory on the land. They make this application in accordance with rules that the government has set down to govern such problems. These rules provide an opportunity for other citizens to make their own needs and desires known. So the other group registers a protest against the factory, requesting that the land be used as a bird sanctuary. Both parties marshal their best arguments and their strongest and most reliable allies to strengthen their demands. Through public hearings or other procedures established by the government, other citizens with an interest in the matter can make themselves and their positions known to the government. All of this bargaining takes place in a marketplace that the government has set up for such matters—perhaps a zoning board or a regional land-use commission.

Throughout the bargaining, governmental rules limit the kinds of arguments and pressures that can be used, the procedures to be followed by the bargaining parties, and even the particular groups or individuals who will be recognized as participants in the bargaining. In some cases, the government may decide that regulations established earlier require a particular decision in the matter. In other cases, the government may render a decision based upon an assessment of the gains and losses that each party would incur from each possible choice in the matter. In any case, the government eventually renders a decision, and informs each party what it may or may not do.

In our example, suppose that the final decision of the zoning board grants permission for construction of a factory on part of the land, but sets aside another part of the land as a bird sanctuary. This leaves no room for a parking lot that had been planned on the site, so the owners will be required to build the parking lot on other land some distance away and provide buses to bring their employees from their cars to the factory. They are also required to observe certain restrictions on the design and operation of the factory that will minimize its effects on the bird sanctuary. The bird lovers, on the other hand, are ordered to accept an area considerably smaller than the one they felt would be desirable to ensure the survival of the bird population.

In most cases, the bargainers recognize that they cannot expect to obtain everything they wanted. Instead, they weigh their gains against their losses to decide whether the outcome is as favorable as they could reasonably expect. If one party is dissatisfied with the decision, he may be allowed by governmental rules to request further rounds of bargaining in some marketplace designated by the government. In our example, the environmentalists might seek a court injunction against the factory construction, claiming that the zoning board acted improperly. They might argue, for example, that the board failed to consider certain pollutants that the factory will emit, and that these pollutants will kill all the birds. Again, governmental rules limit the kinds of arguments that will be accepted and the procedures to be followed in further bargaining. If the environmentalists choose instead to try to block factory construction by direct action, they have stepped outside the bargaining procedures that the government authorizes. The government then will take action to punish them for their interference with the original decision. No matter how strongly they feel about the matter, the government (backed by its authority from the general citizenry) insists that they accept the decisions reached under the government-established procedures of the appropriate bargaining arenas.

In order to understand the bargaining process, we must first determine how to measure the value placed upon the various resources traded in the governmental marketplaces. We can define the *cost* of some result as the total value given up in order to achieve that result (less the value of anything gained in the bargaining process). The economist or accountant limits his consideration of cost to those values that can be reasonably measured in terms of money. However, political bargaining often involves less tangible costs, such as a loss of prestige or the loss to the community of the pleasures to be gained from having a bird sanctuary. Such costs are very difficult to measure in any objective way. Often we can only estimate the value placed upon them by the bargainers by noting the balances reached in the exchange process.

The greater the demand for a given result—tangible or intangible—and the more limited its availability, the higher will be its cost in the political marketplace. If suitable land for factory sites is plentiful in the area, the cost of obtaining permission to build on such a site will be low. If the tract of swampy land we have discussed happens to be the only place in the region suitable for either a factory or a bird sanctuary, the cost of the site will be high for either the factory owner or the environmentalists. The direct cost of the factory site includes the price paid for the land, as well as any money spent in obtaining governmental permission to build the factory there. In our example, it also includes the cost of the off-site parking lot and the bus service for the employees. It may also include such intangible factors as the prestige lost by the company when it opposed the building of a bird sanctuary, or when newspaper stories about the court proceedings portrayed it as a polluter.

In addition to the direct cost, a particular outcome may involve an *opportunity cost*—the value of some other choice given up in order to achieve the present result. For example, the factory owner might have had an opportunity to build a warehouse in another part of town, but gave up that plan in order to devote his time, money, and influence to the fight for the factory site. The lost warehouse then becomes an opportunity cost of the factory site. It must be added to the direct costs of acquiring the site if we are to have a true picture of what the owner gave up in order to get the factory site.

Still another factor might be considered when computing the cost of a result. This is the investment made by the bargainer in order to get himself into a good bargaining position. For example, the environmentalists might have put a lot of time and money into programs designed to make the community aware of the desirability of a bird sanctuary, and the resulting public support may have greatly improved their position in the bargaining over the land. Similarly, the factory owner may have invested his time and money in learning how to design a business that will appeal to the community, how best to present his plan to gain public support, and how best to pursue his case in the political marketplace. All of these costs may contribute to his success in getting permission to build his factory.

Balanced against the cost of a result is the *profit* that the bargainer obtains from the result. Again, political profit includes intangible factors as well as those benefits that can be evaluated directly in terms of money. One aspect of profit is the direct reward obtained through the bargaining—the value of the resources obtained or the actions permitted. The greater the reward, the more likely it is that any random citizen will seek to obtain it. However, with this heavy competition for the reward, there is almost certain to be an increased cost of obtaining it. The higher the cost (even if the reward is very desirable), the less attractive the result becomes to the average citizen. Therefore, the process of bargaining tends to adjust costs and profits in such a way that demand will be adjusted to match supply for any given reward.

The government occupies a unique position in relation to the bargaining process. It can add to the cost factor of certain choices by imposing restrictions, fines, or other deprivations on those who behave in certain ways. It can add to the profit factor of other choices by granting privileges or rewards associated with certain behaviors. In this way, the government can strongly influence the outcomes of the bargaining that goes on in the political marketplace.

Human interaction is, of course, even more complex than our example suggests. For example, past experience plays an important role in the behavior of a bargainer. If the present situation is very similar to some past situation, the individual is likely to be strongly influenced by the rewards or punishments he received in the past encounter; if the factory owner in our example benefited greatly from construction of another similar factory in the past, he is likely to incur a heavier cost in order to build the present factory. Whenever an action is rewarded, the individual is more likely to repeat that action in the future. Other individuals, noting the reward given for the action, also are likely to undertake similar actions. So long as the activity proves rewarding, pursuit of that activity will continue. A heavy demand is created for the resources needed in pursuit of the activity. If any of these resources is limited, the cost of the activity rises in the bargaining process, making it less desirable. The government may step in to further increase the cost if it feels that the bargaining process is not taking account of all costs to the society in the long run.

A further complication arises because the desire for a certain resource may taper off after a certain level has been obtained. For example, the citizens of the community may work very hard to be sure that the bird sanctuary is created, because they want to be sure that some birds are preserved for the enjoyment of themselves and their children. However, the environmentalists might find little support if they tried to prevent the construction of a second factory in order to build a second bird sanctuary. As another example, citizens might pay a high price in order to prevent air pollution that makes them choke and cough. However, they may balk at paying even a low cost to further purify the air once it seems quite breathable. In other words, the value of a given result depends upon the degree to which people already have satisfied the needs or desires associated with that result. The value of any given item in the political marketplace is not a constant; it varies with the extent to which the bargainer's need for that item is already satisfied. We often use the concept of *marginal utility* to describe this effect. The marginal utility of a resource for a bargainer is the cost that he will pay to obtain one more unit of that resource (given the amount of the resource that he has already).

In almost every case, the marginal utility of a resource for an individual decreases as he obtains more of that resource. Usually, the decrease is fairly slow until the individual obtains a certain level of the resource that meets his needs or desires; then the marginal utility drops quite rapidly as more of the resource is obtained. In effect, the individual decides that he would rather spend his money or time to obtain some other resource, now that he has enough of the first one. The constantly shifting marginal utilities of various resources for various individuals adds to the complexity of the political marketplace.

In the economic model, where each cost and profit can be measured fairly precisely in terms of money, the individual is assumed to behave in a highly rational fashion, always maximizing his own profits. The metaphor of political exchange involves a more individualistic, psychological model of human behavior. In this model, cultural factors may be very important parts of the costs and profits involved in a choice, even though they cannot easily be expressed in terms of money. A person may put a very high value on the good opinions of his neighbors. That is, he may avoid a particular action even though the profits seem high if one of the costs is the strong disapproval of others in his social group.

If all parties to a bargaining situation see themselves as having profited from the exchange, the behavior patterns of this exchange are reinforced and are likely to be repeated. This is true even if one of the parties feels that others have profited more than he has. The fact that this pattern is accepted and approved by members of the society can then itself become a reward that helps to perpetuate the pattern.

Some individuals spend valuable time, itself a cost factor, in a continuous search for better alternatives—for behaviors that will yield even greater rewards. However, most of us will stop looking around when we find some behavior pattern that is at least minimally satisfying. We will then continue this pattern as long as it continues to satisfy our basic needs. Apparently, the marginal utility of a change falls off quite rapidly once our minimal needs are satisfied, even though the change might offer a chance for greater profits.

One more factor should be considered before we turn our attention to the processes whereby the individual learns the basic beliefs and values that support the political structure, and that in turn influence the perceptions and expectations upon which the entire system of political exchange is predicated. This additional factor is the cost of the government itself as a facilitator of exchange and a regulator of marketplaces. When we grant authority to the government to regulate our behavior, we give up some of our individual freedom to do whatever we wish. On the one hand, we may resent the fact that government adds the cost of heavy taxes to the profit we might obtain from a small business. On the other hand, we accept the government's power to impose a long prison sentence on someone who robs a business because we recognize the benefit we obtain when others are restrained from robbing us. We pay the costs of government—both the direct costs paid through taxes and the indirect cost of accepting the government's right to limit our behavior—in order to obtain the benefit of having other people restrained in their ability to interfere with our lives.

In other words, the government limits individual choices at the same time that it facilitates the dynamic process of give and take in the political marketplace. The society supports the government so long as the benefits seem to outweigh the costs for any group of individuals with enough power to support or topple the government.

POLITICAL CULTURE AND SOCIALIZATION

The outcomes of political exchanges on all levels depend upon the relative values that bargaining agents assign to various activities, pursuits, and goals. Therefore, students of politics must examine the ways that people develop their attitudes about the values of various alternatives. In any given culture, the majority of people agree quite closely about the values of particular actions or resources. In another culture, the values assigned to these items may be quite different. The process whereby someone internalizes the values and assumptions of his society is called *socialization*. This is the process through which a child acquires the "conscience," learns the set of "dos and don'ts," that permit him to survive or even prosper in his society. If he moves as an adult to a different society, he will feel like an outsider (and be regarded as such) unless he is able to undergo a new process of socialization to internalize the values and assumptions of that society.

Socialization is a dynamic, ongoing process in any society. Children are constantly being indoctrinated into the attitudes, expectations, and value hierarchies of the society. In addition, these structures themselves are constantly changing as the society adapts to new conditions, so that adults within the society must undergo constant socialization to keep up with changing times. Socialization allows each member to gradually accept as his own the entire network of moral precepts, norms of behavior, criteria for critical judgments, and bases for expecting certain outcomes of actions—a network that covers the entire panorama of his life's experiences. Insofar as this process relates to the acquisition of habits, mores, and assumptions that enable the individual to become a functioning participant in the political bargaining process, we can call it political socialization. Our approach to the discussion of socialization emphasizes the rationality of the individual. We do not deny the role of nonrational or irrational influences on individual behavior. However, we are trying to build a simple model that will explain the political process. We find it useful to assume that each person pursues certain goals, and that he tends to take actions that he perceives as enhancing his chances of attaining those goals. We also assume that the person makes some rational balance of costs against profits for any particular action—at least as he perceives those profits and costs. Using this simple model, we then can explain most "nonrational" actions as the result of a person's unusual goals or of his misperception of the costs and profits resulting from a given action. Of course, the nature of the choice that a person makes will depend upon the amount and nature of the information he has about the likely costs and profits to follow upon each possible choice.

Socialization, in our rationalistic model, is a learning process involving a series of exchanges, beginning in infancy, between the individual and his environment. This environment includes parents, other adults, peers, and the educational system established by the society. From this environment, the individual person obtains rewards when he behaves in ways that the society approves or when he expresses attitudes, opinons, beliefs, and values that are shared by members of the society. He receives punishments or deprivations when he behaves in ways that the society disapproves, or when he expresses unacceptable ideas. Because he tends to repeat actions that bring rewards and to avoid those that bring punishments, the person soon adopts the values and beliefs of the society as guides to his own actions. In most cases, he adopts them as his own values and beliefs and is not even aware that they have been learned; he regards them as "natural" human attitudes.

Similar processes of socialization determine individual attitudes about values in all realms of human behavior. In the economic realm, prices provide an objective measure of value. If a pound of steak is selling for $3 and a pound of hamburger for $1 in most markets nearby, then bargainers will readily agree that one pound of steak should be exchanged for three pounds of hamburger in any bargain, even if one person happens to like hamburger just as well as he likes steak. In the political realm, there is no such clear mechanism for comparing the value hierarchies of different people. Consequently, political bargaining often occurs between people who have different hierarchies of values for the alternatives being considered, while this difference in evaluation of costs and profits may not be at all obvious to the bargaining agents.

For example, consider the two goals of liberty and equality. Most Americans today would perceive these goals as very desirable and would assign high values to their achievement. However, particular individuals or groups may differ greatly in the relative values that they assign to the two goals. Black Americans, as a group, do not receive as large a share of the benefits of the society as they would receive if benefits were distributed equally. Therefore, blacks are likely to regard equality as a more valuable goal than liberty. They may be willing to accept some restrictions upon liberty if those restrictions will help achieve equality in the distribution of benefits. They may tend to favor strong actions by centralized government that tend to equalize benefits, regardless of the restrictions this strong central authority may place upon individual liberty. Other groups, who already receive at least their "fair share" of the benefits, may place a higher value upon liberty and a lower value upon equality. They view the demands of the blacks as a threat to their freedom of action—by raising their taxes, for example. The bargaining between the two attitudes in the political marketplace is complicated by this difference in values, and by the fact that neither party may understand the value system being used by the other.

Whatever the differences in individual values and beliefs, the majority of members in a society must share some set of beliefs and values that permits the governmental structures to function. If any powerful segment of the society consistently opposes the actions of the government, some change in the government will be forced. When the society is functioning without such changes in government, its members share some sort of political culture—a totality of beliefs and values that supports the authority of the government. This political culture determines the particular form that the political marketplace will take within the society. This form, in turn, largely determines the modes of political behavior that will be followed by people within the society.

To a large extent, the behavior of individual citizens in the political realm is determined by the shared values of the political culture. This culture attaches symbols of worth or worthlessness to various possible achievements and actions; it informs people as to what is worthy of pursuit and what is not, the areas in which they should compete, and the goals on which they should expend their resources.

Although the relative values and expectations—along with the norms that stabilize the political system—vary from one society to another, the general model can be applied to any culture. This model of a political system can be applied to any human society to explain individual and collective decision making, whether individuals are conscious of the political structure or not, and whether the society is traditional and homogeneous or industrial and heterogeneous. The universal model of culturally designated modes of exchange accounting for forms of political behavior can help us understand political stability as a product of reinforcement or political change as a result of satiation with previous rewards and a search for new alternatives.

From society to society, we find a diversity of political cultures. These cultures vary in the amount of respect that citizens have for political authority, in the extent to which citizens insist upon freedom to make their own decisions, in the particular areas where they will acquiesce in the demands of others (or refuse to do so), and in the manner in which they demonstrate respect or disrespect for a person, an office, or a decision. For example, in some nations military leaders exercise unquestioned authority; in others, any attempt at military domination is regarded with great skepticism or hostility by the populace. Many cultural distinctions can be explained in terms of traditions within particular societies. Political traditions reflect historical experiences, some of which proved rewarding while others proved overly costly for the society. Political tradition also reflects the economic systems and religious beliefs on which the culture is founded. Such systems and beliefs greatly affect the types of political institutions developed in the society, and the styles of exercising political authority that will be accepted.

Political culture, then, permeates every aspect of life. It both reflects and influences every segment of society. This pervasive force generates and maintains those values that tend to keep the society's particular way of life intact. The diversity among political cultures may be diminishing in the modern age of sophisticated telecommunications and travel. Despite the diversity that does exist, however, the processes by which a political culture originates, operates, and affects the society—as well as the dynamic process of interaction among the political culture, societal values, and individual behavior patterns—are similar the world over.

The concept of political culture helps us to explain the origin of those beliefs and values that motivate certain forms of individual action, discourage certain other forms of action, and establish at least a rough "price list" setting forth agreed values for many kinds of symbols—both tangible and intangible, both real and imagined—so that political exchange can take place. People learn from previous events which of their possible investments will bring high rewards from others when exchanged within their society. Thus, a young person is willing to pursue a difficult training program at great personal cost in order to acquire a rare skill that is in high demand in his culture. When he completes the training program, he can offer this skill to other members of the society and receive high rewards in return. The greater his personal investment in training, the greater the reward he will expect when he finally is ready to exercise the skill he has acquired. Suppose that the rewards are not as great as he expected—perhaps because demand for the skill has diminished in the society, or perhaps because the supply of persons trained in this skill has greatly increased. In this case, the person is likely to feel that he has been the victim of an injustice, and he will become angry. The sense of a "just reward" or "fair play" is also a learned value, based upon personal and cultural past experiences.

From the preceding example, we see that exchanges involve more than goods and services. Such factors as esteem and approval are included in the bargaining, although the bargainers may not be consciously aware of the role these factors play in their exchanges. The concept of justice is not identical from one society to another, but some form of this concept seems to play an important role in keeping any culture intact and functioning. Anger seems to be an almost universal response when an individual feels himself the victim of an injustice. The greater the discrepancy between what he actually received and what he expected as a just reward, the more likely he is to display his anger—although the form in which he expresses anger will be influenced by cultural traditions. He might express his anger by taking aggressive action against the person responsible for the injustice. However, this direct response may be discouraged by cultural factors. For example, in our culture it is risky to act aggressively toward one's superior. In such a case, the wronged person often seems to find some release for anger in behaving aggressively toward some other person who is not in a position to punish the behavior. The brunt of someone's anger may fall on a husband or wife or children, or on some outsider. It may well become a factor in some other bargaining exchange. This sort of factor in political exchanges often is neither rational nor conscious.

Values are not only different between cultures; they also change over time within a single culture. The balance between supply and demand for a resource may change, for obvious reasons such as an increase in available supply, or for more subtle reasons such as a shift in "tastes." The idea of a just return for a given contribution may also change. People often retain the set of values and the sense of fair play that prevailed during their childhoods—the time when they internalized the values of the society around them. Thus, shifts in the realities of the marketplace may lead to different expectations on the part of different members of the same society. One participant in an exchange may feel that he is treating the other justly, while the other feels outraged at the way he is being treated. Such differing expectations can greatly complicate the process of political exchange.

Suppose that one citizen perceives an injustice being done against his neighbor. If he regards his own condition as similar to that of the neighbor, he is likely to feel a sense of outrage almost as strong as he would feel if the injustice were done to him. He feels, perhaps unconsciously, that the same sort of injustice could just as well happen to him. His sense of security and stability within the society depends upon his belief that standards of justice prevail in the marketplace. Therefore, he is likely to be almost as upset if the neighbor receives a reward that he perceives as in excess of his just due. In such a case, the neighbor also is apt to be discomforted, feeling somewhat guilty for having received this reward that his friend regards as unmerited. All of these emotions are apt to influence future exchanges, perhaps even exchanges that seem totally unrelated to the incident that provoked the emotions.

Still another source of complexity is the time gap that often exists between an action and its reward or punishment. We have mentioned the young person who embarks upon a training program in expectation of future compensation. Another example would be someone who undertakes charitable activities, expecting no immediate reward but probably expecting some future return in the form of approval or praise. If the expected reward is never received, the person may feel angry. He is likely to discontinue the activities that brought little reward; others, seeing what happened, may also avoid those activities. In order to understand the behavior of people, therefore, we must look not only at the actual benefits exchanged in the marketplace but also at the highly subjective perceptions and motivations of the participants in the exchange.

In a heterogeneous and complex society, such as the contemporary United States, it may be difficult to define a single political culture. Although some values and beliefs do generally prevail in the U.S., political behavior can best be understood by viewing the society in terms of numerous subcultures. These subcultures share some beliefs and values basic to the society in general. With their different past experiences, family and social arrangements, religions, and so on, these diverse subcultures may hold differing hierarchies of values and differing perceptions of needs. Each subculture produces a different market context with its own set of expectations and sense of justice.

Some of these political subcultures tend to prevail in the national political marketplaces. The more that a given person feels detached from the prevailing political sector—feeling that his behavior is unaffected and his actions unrewarded by the governmental structure—the less likely he is to be politically aware and active, or to change his behavior patterns in response to the pattern of rewards and punishments that the government imposes. At the other extreme, someone from a subculture that strongly influences the national marketplaces has confidence that he will be rewarded for the actions that seem appropriate and proper to him; he believes that his actions will have a marked impact on governmental decisions, and he in turn is strongly influenced by the government's imposition of rewards and punishments. If reality bears out his expectations, his patterns of behavior are reinforced. Meanwhile, the person from the minority subculture is likely to find that he gets no reinforcement when he acts in ways that seem worthy of reward to him. He grows more isolated from the government. Thus, the patterns of reinforcement tend to enhance the dominant position of the prevailing subcultures, and to drive isolated subcultures further into isolation.

In all of these comments about the nature of the political process, we find that socialization plays a central role. Through socialization, the political culture is constantly being transmitted to new members of the society. Only through a careful study of this interaction between the political culture and the individual human being can we understand the give and take that we label as political behavior.

Research reveals that children learn political values—or at least the basic values and attitudes from which political values and behavior patterns will later emerge—at an early age and in much the same manner that small children develop other value, belief, and ethical systems. The original source and the major impact comes from the parents (or those individuals who act as the child's parents). During childhood, other family members, friends, and neighbors may have some influence upon the child's beliefs. Still later, further contributions come from other children, the educational system, and adults in positions of high status—both those met directly and those encountered through books, movies, television, and so on. At various times during his life, the individual may identify himself with actual or imagined groups—neighborhoods, religions, professional groups, social groups, and so on. The influence of each may reinforce or modify the belief and value structure internalized earlier. And, of course, particular beliefs and values are constantly being reinforced or weakened by the results of the individual's own actions.

Thus we see that the process of political socialization continues throughout the lifetime of an individual; his beliefs and values are constantly being tested against and modified by the realities of the society around him. Nonetheless, the influences absorbed during childhood remain very strong in most cases. An infant forms many beliefs and values long before he has any political awareness. These influences, absorbed at an early age, often are not accessible to his rational awareness, yet they continue to affect his behavior as an adult. We have already mentioned the tendency for individuals raised in some subcultures to regard the political process as meaningless and foreign, while those raised in other subcultures naturally acquire a high degree of political awareness and readily participate in the political process. The more that the various socializing influences reinforce one another, the stronger will be the individual's orientation toward the political world, whether that attitude is positive or negative. Conversely, the more that the various influences contradict one another, the more likely it is that the individual will be indecisive, vacillating, and confused about the political process. The various beliefs and values that he has absorbed contradict one another, pushing him in various directions siumltaneously, making it difficult for him to perceive any clear choice. We say that such an individual is cross-pressured; he is likely to be very ambivalent in his attitudes and actions in the political realm.

The student of politics must always be aware of the fact that each individual perceives the political process in terms of his own unique structure of values and beliefs—a structure that is the cumulative result of all the various socializing influences acting upon him throughout his life. Two individuals may show the same overt political behavior, but it is very likely that they will have differing views of how and why they are acting. Both may be very surprised when they find themselves following different behavior patterns in some other situation—and so would be the political scientist *if* he assumed that individuals acting in the same way in one particular situation must share the same belief and value structure. Walter Lippmann, a scholar of political behavior, pointed out in 1922 the importance of the fact that people's actions in reality are based upon their own individual perceptions of that reality. It is a fact that we must keep firmly in mind throughout our study.

REFERENCES

Aristotle. *Politics*. Translated by Ernest Barker. New York: Oxford, 1962.

Dahl, Robert A. *Modern Political Analysis*. Englewood Cliffs, N.J.: Prentice-Hall, 1963.

Waldman, Sidney R. *Foundations of Political Action*. Boston: Little, Brown, 1972.

Those Lingering Questions 2 CHAPTER

LEGITIMACY

The function of a government is to establish structures that can produce authoritative decisions. These decisions facilitate exchanges,
discourage undesirable behavior, and disseminate a viable set of
ground rules for players in the game of politics. These goals can be
achieved only if there is a consensus, a minimal agreement among a
sufficiently large proportion of the citizens, giving authority to the
government. When the citizens regard the government's authoritative
actions as rightful behavior, the government is said to have *legitimacy*. The government tells a citizen what to do (on the basis of its
official position), and the citizen usually acquiesces. He recognizes
the authority of the government to direct him, even if he disagrees with
the particular decision. Such a grant of authority by the citizens
often is based upon a tradition going back over generations. In such

cases, the tradition obviously must have been reinforced because individual citizens received benefits sufficient to cause them to keep supporting the authority of the government.

In some cases, the members of a society grant legitimacy to a new form of government, or to one that differs considerably from the form traditionally recognized in that society. Obviously, support for the authority of the new government has not been reinforced by past experience. Rather, the support must be based upon the citizens' belief that they will receive benefits from the new government exceeding the reinforcements they obtained for supporting the traditional government. In most cases, legitimacy is granted to a new government only when there is a high level of dissatisfaction with the benefits obtained from the old government.

Consider, for example, the drastic changes in government that ensued when Hitler became chancellor of Germany in 1933. The German people granted legitimacy to Hitler's exercise of dictatorial powers, even though the Nazi government differed drastically from the Weimar Republic that had existed previously. In large part, the Germans were ready to believe that the Nazi government could benefit them because they had suffered severely during the years after World War I and the depression under the Weimar government. The legitimacy of the Weimar government also was somewhat shaky because it had been established as part of the settlement of World War I, and many Germans viewed the government as one imposed upon them by their conquerors. Furthermore, Hitler had been chancellor under the old government, and his original powers as a dictator were approved by the cabinet after the death of President Hindenberg; thus his initial seizure of power had at least some appearance of legitimacy under the forms of the old government. Finally, many scholars have argued that an important factor was the German tradition of granting unquestioned authority to those in power, a tradition that may have survived undiminished through the brief 15-year existence of the republican government. This example also emphasizes the fact that a government can achieve legitimacy without the complete support of all citizens. Many Germans opposed the Nazi government, and a sizeable number refused to recognize its authority. However, the government obtained support from a sufficient proportion of the population to permit it to function as a legitimate government. Legitimacy, in the sense we use it, implies nothing about the moral or ethical nature of the government; it implies only that the government has enough support from its citizens that it can function as the arbiter for political bargaining within the society.

Suppose that a member of the society feels that he is being hurt more than he is helped by the actions of the government. If his internal set of values includes a strong belief in his duty to obey the existing government, he may continue to recognize the legitimacy of the government. In effect, he places a higher value upon the maintenance of traditional governmental order than he does upon his own personal gains or losses. However, this person could also decide that he will no longer obey governmental policy, that he will oppose the authority of the government. The government is no longer legitimate in the eyes of this person. Such a decision is not taken lightly, for the person risks losing any benefits offered by the present system and incurring the punishments that the government decrees for those who defy its decisions. So long as the person feels that he may eventually obtain benefits from the existing government (or perhaps that his children may), he is likely to submit to governmental authority and to seek success within the existing structure.

The dissatisfied person might find a place in a subculture that views itself as isolated from the governmental structures and from the behavior norms that prevail in the society. The lifestyle of such a subculture could be called asystemic; that is, its members tend to operate outside of the rules established by the dominant subcultures. The existence of an asystemic subculture is often tolerated by the government if its members do not openly violate rules that are considered important by the government. Its members may obtain some benefits from the official structure, in return for their tacit agreement not to interfere with the government's authority over the major part of the population. The "hippy" or "dropout" subculture of the past decade or so could be regarded as such a subculture. Its members may obtain some benefits such as welfare payments from the official structure, and (except for relatively minor harassment) the government may overlook minor violations of its rules because it realizes that the subculture does not seriously threaten the legitimacy of its rule over the main part of the society.

If the dissatisfied person fails to find satisfaction in an asystemic subculture, he may become an active opponent of the government, either on his own or in company with a group of other dissatisfied persons. He may become a criminal, seeking to defy laws for the sake of his own gain and to avoid the punishment that the government decrees for such actions. On the other hand, he may defy the government yet accept its punishment as an act of witness against it. If he sees his goal as the overthrow of the government (and the establishment of a new government that will offer greater benefits), he is likely to consider himself a revolutionary. The government (and those who recognize the legitimacy of the government) are likely to treat such defiant opponents simply as criminals, granting them no political legitimacy.

So long as strong discontent with the government is manifested by a tolerable minority of the population, the political system can survive because a sufficient consensus of legitimacy still exists. As we have said, the government can use its authority to impose punishments upon those who defy it—depriving them of things they want and need, including liberty. Such governmental punishments serve both to make it less likely that the offenders will repeat their undesirable actions and to warn other members of the society that unpleasant consequences will follow if they do likewise.

The criminal persists in his behavior because he believes that his actions will lead to rewards greater than those he could obtain by following the rules laid down by the government. In short, the chance of gains outweighs the risk of punishment in his view. However, the individual who defies the government because of a strongly held belief operates upon a different motivation. The satisfaction that he obtains from remaining true to his own beliefs is sufficient to balance the threat (or actuality) of punishment imposed by the government. Harsher rules and punishments are unlikely to reduce his motivation to oppose an unjust government.

Questions about the continuing viability of the political system arise if a significant portion of the citizenry chooses to defy the authority of the government. Sometimes such a challenge arises because of a single governmental action that is inconsistent with the desires of many individuals, or that violates the ethical standards of a large or powerful subculture. In such a case, the government can regain its legitimacy by backtracking and changing its policy. The institution and subsequent removal of prohibition in the United States provides an example of this process. During prohibition, a significant portion of the population supported groups that defied the government to distribute and sell alcohol. Although the government realized its error and repealed prohibition, it has not yet succeeded in eliminating the antisystemic organization that was originally created to supply the alcohol demanded by the population during prohibition.

When the challenge to governmental authority by a significant group in the society involves opposition to a major part of the system of policies and laws that make up the political system, the government faces a much more serious disruption of its legitimacy. In effect, the members of the society are saying that the government's use of its power in distributing scarce resources is unjust and inequitable. Such massive disagreement and disobedience indicate a widespread questioning of the basic values that form and maintain the political system. No simple revision of minor parts of the system will restore the legitimacy of the government in the eyes of the citizens. A significant portion of the society feels that it stands to lose more than it will gain by following the rules laid down by the government. These individuals seek alternatives that will restore a just balance to the political marketplace.

In such a situation, the population is likely to grant legitimacy to some new government that arises to challenge the old. The transition might occur through a revolution, or it might occur through a less violent seizure of power by those who offer a new governmental structure that the citizens perceive as beneficial. Note that the significant factor here is the way that members of the society perceive the balance of gains and losses in the existing system as opposed to that they expect under some proposed new system. Although we may be certain that the German people erred in granting legitimacy to Hitler, we will achieve an understanding of the political process only if we seek to understand the perceptions that led them to grant him that legitimacy.

In the exchanges that take place between those who govern and those who are governed, individuals must achieve minimal satisfaction of certain basic needs and desires. They will then give up personal options and allow governmental authority to make crucial choices affecting them. If minimal satisfaction is not achieved, the citizens may simply avoid participation in the systems set up by the government. In that case, new systems are created and the give and take between individuals or groups is carried on in marketplaces outside the governmental ones. The authority of the government then becomes relatively meaningless, and the effective governing role is filled by other individuals or groups. Legitimacy, then, is a positive force that is destroyed by apathy and alienation as well as by active opposition. Legitimacy is essential to any effective form of government.

SOCIAL MOVEMENTS AND SOCIAL CHANGE

The visualization of politics as an operating system is a useful model of the dynamic give and take that constitutes the policy-making aspect of society. The system metaphor is a universal model, applicable to diverse types of political culture. Operating within the rules established by the particular political culture, groups and individuals apply pressure on the decision-making apparatus in an attempt to obtain decisions that they regard as favorable. The action of the government is influenced not only by the balance of pressures applied to it, but by its own structure—that is, by the decisionmakers' own views of options, needs, costs, and ramifications. Depending upon the way the government is constructed, certain kinds of decisions may be likely only under extreme pressures. For example, in the United States governmental structure, it is relatively easy to create a new project, commission, bureau, or department in response to some demand from the citizenry; it is much more difficult to abolish an existing element of the governmental apparatus.

Whenever citizens look to the government for a decision on some matter, the government must respond in some way. In most cases, the decision is some sort of compromise that seeks to give some satisfaction to the various groups putting pressure upon the government. Even a decision to delay (or an ambiguous decision) is a significant action by the government—in effect, a decision to postpone final resolution of the issue.

When the parties involved in the issue become aware of the government's decision, each will react with some degree of pleasure or displeasure. As we have seen, the overall balance of this reaction is extremely crucial to the stability of the system. Because most resources are limited, it is seldom possible for the government to fully satisfy all citizens with a particular decision. However, if the government is to retain its legitimacy, a sizeable portion of the population must continue to be satisfied with the overall pattern of governmental action. Then and only then will the political culture remain intact. If too many members of the society begin to view the government's actions as unjust or damaging to their welfare, the forces opposing governmental authority will become strong enough to disrupt the normal functioning of the political system. The resultant chaos in the operation of the society will create an overwhelming demand for a new governmental structure that can restore orderly operations in the political marketplaces.

The processes by which new values and systems of values emerge are complex. Social scientists do not fully understand these processes, and no adequate theories exist to explain such changes. Many of the significant variables affecting these changes have been identified, but we do not know which of these variables are most important or how they interact. However, history does provide enough material to support some speculation about the causes of value change, and the exchange metaphor gives us a conceptual framework for imposing structure on the data. Throughout history, value changes appear to have been byproducts of changes in modes of production, levels of technology, or shifts in demography—or the results of forces such as imperialism and colonialism. Whatever the triggering forces, the emergence of a new set of values in a culture reflects many changes in the value hierarchies of individual members of that culture. These changes both reflect and trigger changes in the cost and supply of needed goods and services.

Even the most casual observer of current events must be aware that this is a time of dramatic and extensive social change. The lack of stability has become almost an accepted part of political life. Various forms of social disruption have been experienced in a wide variety of political cultures, including many that had remained extremely stable for generations. We grant that "social change" is a vague term, but we use it deliberately to encompass a wide variety of upheavals in the patterns and structures that enable a society to function from day to day. Depending upon the nature of the change and your own value system, you may view a particular change as anything from dangerous to necessary. As observers of political behavior, however, we are interested in the process by which fundamental change occurs in the value system or governmental structure of a society. A change may be relatively gradual and orderly, or it may be sudden and violent. In either form, social change can restructure power relationships within the society, alter the network of economic and social groupings, and even modify the underlying philosophy of the entire society. A study of the causes and the processes of social change will help us understand contemporary politics. An important part of this study is a search for the role of ideologies and social movements in the process of change.

If the primary function of the political system is to convert the needs and desires of people into practical policy that fulfills those needs and desires, then change in its broadest sense can best be viewed as the making of adjustments needed to keep the system functioning as the requirements of the population vary. Many political systems have built-in mechanisms for making changes, so that minor dissatisfactions with the government can be made known immediately in a nondisruptive and constructive manner. Such mechanisms also provide for changes in details of the governmental structure or for replacement of particular decisionmakers without greatly altering the basic rules and structures of the political culture. The constitutional democracies of the modern world, for example, experience periodic change that is accomplished through electoral processes whose exact nature varies from one society to another. Over many years, the cumulative effects of these minor changes may significantly alter the governmental structure and the political values of the culture. The possibility of such change produced by actions within the rules of the system makes the alternative of antisystemic action much less attractive. Citizens feel able to express discontent, frustration, or even anger in meaningful ways without denying the legitimacy of the government. The majority of the populace is likely to oppose any individual or group that resorts to violence or other antisystemic behavior. Of course, many individuals within such a country may be dissatisfied with the current actions of their government. However, they are likely to believe that they can remedy the problem through changes that they can bring about while operating within the rules of the political system.

Antisystemic action involves a large investment of personal resources and a high risk of unpleasant consequences. Actions aimed at producing change within the rules of the system require less risk and often seem to offer a higher probability of a rewarding return. For example, an American citizen is likely to join (or help form) an organized pressure group in order to stimulate change within the limits of what is considered acceptable and legitimate political behavior in the culture. Such action appears both more effective and less risky than, say, an isolated act of wanton destruction as a protest against some perceived injustice.

We have mentioned the existence of asystemic subcultures and individuals who view the political structure as unresponsive to their needs or unjust in its actions, so they carry on their lives outside the marketplaces established by the government. If they do not violate major rules of the political system but simply avoid taking part in the political exchanges of the society, the government may tolerate (or even encourage) the existence of asystemic subcultures because they seem to offer a harmless alternative that diverts dissatisfied individuals from antisystemic action. However, the asystemic individual or group may eventually become a problem for the political culture.

The asystemic individual receives little reinforcement for acting in ways that the government approves. As time passes, he comes to feel more and more detached from the governmental system. If he is reinforced within the subculture for violating some minor governmental rules, he may be encouraged to take antisystemic actions. Playing by different rules, so to speak, such individuals or groups may resort to unaccepted or illegal methods in order to achieve a more beneficial distribution of the goods and services that they desire from the society. Should these methods produce beneficial results, the antisystemic approach will be reinforced, both for those who used it and for other alienated individuals or groups who observe the action and its results. If the antisystemic methods fail—assuming that the mere exercise in rebellious behavior was not rewarding in itself as a release for pent-up hostility—then a greater investment will be made in the search for alternative course of action. Because the alienated individual has come to view the political system as irrelevant or even hostile, it is possible that his search for alternatives will turn toward even more extreme antisystemic behaviors.

The term *ideology* is often used to describe the set of beliefs, ethical tenets, and values shared by the members of a culture or subculture. The ideology determines the assumptions and goals that will gain general approval within the society. For example, the ideology of some cultures includes the belief that it is morally proper to save and invest as much money as possible rather than spending it on unnecessary personal consumption. A high level of investment among the population may be important in helping a country to industrialize, because it helps provide funds for capital improvements. Therefore, a country whose ideology puts a positive value upon individual thriftiness may have an edge in the industrialization process over some other country where the ideology praises lavish personal consumption.

For a group seeking to restructure the society radically, a counterculture ideology may serve much the same purpose. Because it causes members of the group to give approval to certain kinds of statements and actions, it can shift the effective balance between reinforcement and punishment, thus leading members of the social movement to behave very differently from the ways that the government has ordained in its rules and laws. For example, the ideology of an antisystemic subculture might give high esteem to individuals who have been punished by the government for acts aimed at changing the political system. Those who share this ideology are unlikely to be deterred from antisystemic actions by threats of governmental punishments. If the ideology of the subculture values certain political goals, however described, above individual lives, members of the group are likely to be willing to undertake violent actions aimed at achieving those goals. Whether violent or nonviolent, a social movement or antisystemic subculture with an ideology of its own may become a very serious threat to the stability of the existing government, because its members are largely immune to governmental sanctions short of direct physical restraint.

REVOLUTION

The more complex a society, the more likely it is that a member of that society will identify himself primarily with one or more smaller groups rather than with the society as a whole. He is likely to describe his political values and objectives by saying that he is a working man, a conservative, a Democrat, a socialist, or a black—rather than saying that he is an American citizen. The different interests in such a pluralistic society are often in conflict with one another, but they must form temporary and shifting coalitions in order to attain sufficient power to influence government.

When an agreement is made between two or more parties, the results of the agreement are likely to have effects (either positive or negative) upon other parties who did not participate in the bargaining. For example, when labor and management in a particular industry agree upon a wage increase, consumers may be subjected to a price increase as a result of the agreement. Such an impact upon a party outside of the agreement is called an *externality*. The government may have to act in its role as arbiter of the marketplace in order to regulate agreements in accordance with their externalities, because the bargaining parties may have no other reason to consider them. Thus, government has stepped in to issue regulations about pollution, because pollution effects have largely been externalities to agreements between industry and its consumers or employees. The bargaining process has not taken adequate account of the effects of its decisions upon the society at large.

If the government does not effectively regulate externalities in the political marketplace, individuals are likely to feel more and more that they lack any voice in important decisions affecting their welfare. As we have seen, alienated individuals are unlikely to participate in the affairs of the political marketplace or to be influenced by the behavioral norms that the government tries to establish. If many citizens feel such alienation from the system, the government may lose its legitimacy simply because other decision-making structures replace it in the practical lives of its citizens. Groups that were originally asystemic may in time come to fill the roles of government for their members.

However, it is quite likely that at least some alienated people will form subcultures that seek to alter the entire socioeconomic distribution of power. If the individual members of such groups have never internalized the culture's standards about change within the existing system—or if they have lost faith in the viability of the system's mechanisms for peaceful change—these groups may seek to alter the system through extralegal means. Particularly if the ideology of the subculture favors a view of the existing system as immoral or unjust, its members are likely to work toward permanent and drastic changes in the system, using methods that the system regards as improper. Such a group, of course, is working toward a revolution in the political system. The agreement among members of the group to try to produce a revolution obviously involves very extreme externalities for all other members of the society.

There are many conditions that may create the potential for a significant revolutionary movement within a society. Many scholars have pointed out that a society becomes very unstable if those in positions of governmental power hold viewpoints that are significantly different from the viewpoints of those with economic power. Other extreme disparities in viewpoints can lead to political instability, such as differences between the general population and the governing elite, or between those who hold positions of authority and those who wield actual power in the day-to-day operation of the system. Furthermore, even the most stable of governmental systems may be disrupted by external factors such as rapid technological change, the effects of worldwide economic shifts, or the dislocation of families during periods of heightened urbanization. If a government fails to respond quickly enough to new expectations of large portions of the population, it can quickly lose legitimacy, even though a long-standing tradition of support for the political system has developed through previous periods of less drastic change.

As more and more people come to feel that the political system is not responding to their needs and demands, frustration increases. This frustration may remain below the threshold of expression for some time, but it is there to fuel an aggressive outpouring of antisystemic action if triggered. The trigger might be a particularly dramatic example of the government's failure to respond, or it might be the emergence of a revolutionary movement that seems to offer a better chance for attaining the goals of the people. The more inflexible the political system, the more rigid its structures and institutions, the less responsive it will be to such political crises, and the greater the likelihood of a revolution.

Another source of social upheaval is cultural misperception, which can occur both in international relations and within a given society. A large group operating outside of the constraints of the political system may wish to make a demand of the decisionmakers. Because the group is unaware of the nuances of the political culture and processes, it may well apply pressure in some fashion that the system does not recognize as legitimate. The demands of the group may be ignored, or worse they may be misinterpreted and answered with governmental sanctions. The group's reaction to this response will probably include frustration, confusion, and some degree of anger directed at the system itself. Unless the problem is recognized and solved, further interactions are likely to lead quickly to a viewpoint on both sides that the group is antisystemic.

The likelihood of such cultural misperception is high both in a complex society with many subcultures and in a society with a relatively new political system whose structure is not well understood by all members of the society. In the case of a young political system, the probability of revolution is further increased by the fact that the system has not yet built up a tradition of popular support, a history of past rewards that reinforce support for the system even when its current decisions seem unfair. Thus, political revolutions are least likely in societies where the political system has existed for a long time and provides flexible mechanisms for change within the rules of the system. However, once a revolution does occur in such a society, the probability of further revolutions against the new government becomes quite high.

It seems logical that support for revolutions would be greatest among those members of any society who have the least to lose and the most to gain by a change in political systems—in short, among the poor and powerless. However, history shows clearly that large groups within a society will endure extreme poverty and lack of power for long periods of time without any strong tendency toward revolution. The leaders of most revolutionary movements have come from more privileged groups within their societies, and these leaders often find it very difficult to arouse support for a revolution among the portion of the population that would supposedly benefit most by it. Apparently a desire for revolution comes when hopes of improvement are stimulated and then frustrated. If a particular group or subculture has been poor and powerless for as long as its members can recall, their mood is likely to be one of despair. They regard themselves as powerless and do not even consider the possibility that their needs might be met under some revised system—or that they could help bring about any change in the system. Revolution is possible only when some factor intervenes to change this despairing acquiescence into an angry demand for a different system.

We are using the term revolution to describe any significant restructuring of the sociopolitical and economic system that is brought about through processes not accepted as legitimate by that system. It need not involve violent battles, although it often does. We have distinguished revolution both from evolutionary systemic change through accepted mechanisms and from isolated antisystemic acts that have no significant effect upon the distribution of power. We should also distinguish it from extralegal changes within the elite (such as coups d'etat) that have no significant effect upon basic social relationships.

VOTING: A CASE STUDY

The act of voting is of particular interest to the political scientist because it provides the most observable example of interaction between individual citizens and the political structure. In many societies, citizens vote frequently on a wide range of questions, and the results of this voting are tabulated and made available for study. The act of voting gives us a concrete example of the individual citizen responding to stimuli, making decisions, and finally either acting or choosing not to. It provides a useful and illuminating case study of political behavior—of the acquisition of political mores and of their use in the marketplace of a given society.

Why does a particular citizen decide to vote or to abstain from voting? If he decides to vote, what are the factors that lead him to vote one way rather than another? What causes a voter to change his mind during the course of a campaign or to change his voting habits from one election to the next? Why does he choose to split his ticket or to vote for one party on all questions? What factors lead him to support or to oppose a local referendum? Studies of these and similar questions provide many insights into the nature of the political process.

In a liberal democracy, a high voting turnout among the citizenry is considered to be a significant indicator of the health of the political system, because political participation is assumed to be essential to the proper functioning of the democracy. Most political studies also assume that the act of voting is an indication that the individual citizen views himself as an active participant in the political system. If the individual feels, on the basis of past experience, that the results of elections do influence the decisions of the government and that the efforts of individuals like himself can affect the results of elections, then he will be motivated to participate in the electoral process. The minimum level of participation requires the effort needed to register and vote. If the citizen is more highly motivated, he may put more of his time, energy, and resources into the process by studying the issues involved in the election, making contributions to campaigns, or actively working to help create support for a candidate, party, or position on some issue. If his effort is not rewarded by some sense of accomplishment, he is likely to make less of an investment in future elections.

The voter (or potential voter) is a prospective participant in an exchange relationship. Through party platforms, speeches, statements of position, and personal contacts, the various candidates promise various benefits that will accrue to him if he invests his vote in their cause. Additional benefits (such as positions in the governmental structure) may be offered to induce the citizen to give active personal or financial support to the campaign. Completing the bargaining cycle, the prospective voter makes his various needs and demands known to the candidates, usually through organized pressure groups and the machinery of political parties. During the course of a preelection campaign, this bargaining process may lead to shifts of position by both the candidates and the prospective voters.

Rarely is the prospective voter able to find a candidate or party that believably promises him everything he wants. In a pluralistic culture such as the United States, there are too many competing interests clearly visible for any voter to take seriously a promise that his own demands will be met totally. In the contemporary electoral process, the mass media allow the urban dwellers to see and hear exactly what a candidate is promising when he woos the farm vote, to make laborers aware of his commitments to management, and so on. If a candidate tries to promise everything to everyone, the contradictions in his proposed policies quickly become apparent to all interest groups. His promises lose credibility on all sides—and because what he can offer in the political bargaining is only his promise of future actions, he no longer has anything to offer to the prospective voters who are shopping for the best place to invest their votes.

The study of voter expectations plays a very crucial part in understanding political behavior. The citizen gives his vote to some particular candidate or position because he expects to gain certain benefits in the future if that candidate or position wins the election. He will not be motivated to cast his vote if he loses faith in the prospect that those benefits will actually be forthcoming. If a candidate loses credibility with the voters, then further promises will do him no good because they will not be believed. He will find it almost impossible to regain popularity once he has lost it. In order to understand the political bargaining process in a particular election, we must look not only at the promises made by the various candidates, but also at the expectations of the voters about what those candidates will actually do if elected.

Voting behavior illustrates the way that the political system seeks to insure its own stability by inculcating in the citizenry a sense of commitment to the system, of personal investment in the society's future, and of faith that the government will be responsive to their needs and desires. So long as the citizens hold these beliefs, the political system will function within legal limits. Dissatisfied individuals will not seek to overthrow the system itself. Instead, they will organize their efforts to elect certain candidates and defeat others, thus working for changes within the limits of the system itself. Even if their efforts fail in the present election, they will view the results as fair and just. They will postpone the satisfaction of their demands and will work with renewed effort toward success in a future election. Only when a significant proportion of the citizenry loses this faith will there be a threat of revolutionary actions aimed at the disruption of the system.

We must be cautious, however, about assuming that participation in the electoral process can uncritically be taken as a sign of faith in the political system. It is true that a citizen will vote only if he expects some reward for doing so (or if he is avoiding some unpleasant result of not doing so). However, the expectation of benefits to be obtained by electing certain candidates is not the only possible motivation for voting. For example, a person may have been socialized in a subculture where voting is regarded as a ceremonial act to be performed by any responsible member of the society. Such a person may vote—or even take an active part in political campaigns—in order to obtain the reward of respect and approval from his peers, even though he may expect to gain nothing at all from the outcome of the political process itself. If he later moves into a different subculture, he may continue to vote simply as a habit—much as some people continue to attend church on religious holidays, even though the ceremony itself holds little meaning for them.

A sudden upsurge in voting among a previously apathetic segment of the population might indicate that the group has been assimilated into the political culture and has internalized the values of the political system. The upsurge might also indicate that this group was previously sufficiently content with its lot to be asystemic, but has now become sufficiently frustrated and angry to take action to press its demands upon the system. The upsurge in voting suggests that the group is willing to try to obtain its goals by acting within the system, but this participation could easily be shortlived. The group has no strong tradition of adherence to the political process, so it is likely to become even more frustrated and angry if its voting activity does not bring benefits fairly quickly. If the group perceives no rewards for its participation within a very few elections, it may turn to antisystemic actions to achieve its demands—particularly if its hopes and expectations have been greatly heightened by the promises of political candidates. Thus, the upsurge in voting may actually be a warning of potential future instability rather than a sign that the political system is functioning more smoothly then ever.

It is very important to examine the attitudes of voters and the ways that these attitudes are formed. Many cultural and individual factors mesh into the final act of voting. As already mentioned, the act of voting or of abstaining from voting may in itself be influenced by a wide variety of cultural values and pressures. A failure to vote may indicate a rejection of the idea that the vote would have any significant effect upon the decision-making machinery of the government, or it may indicate that the individual's value system does not emphasize the desirability or importance of voting. In a subculture where voting is not a highly regarded activity, other forms of political activity such as active membership in organizations may be encouraged as a way of participating in the political marketplace.

A person develops his attitude structure, his hierarchy of values, and his basic assumptions about life under the influence of socializing agents such as family, peers, neighborhood, school, and church—starting at a very early age. His voting attitudes are formed as part of this socialization. Whether or not an individual will vote, will identify with a political party, or will participate in a campaign are behaviors determined to a large extent by the specific environment in which the individual was nurtured. In a pluralistic culture such as the United States, different individuals grow up in a wide variety of political environments. Thus, the citizens form a wide variety of basic attitudes toward politics—attitudes that may be modified by later experiences, but that are difficult to discard altogether. Indeed, it is a very traumatic experience if an individual's fundamental ideas are shattered by the realities around him. To avoid this trauma, a person is likely to be selective in what he perceives, failing even to become aware of things that would conflict with his basic beliefs. The voter therefore views political reality through a perceptual grid that filters out any aspects of reality that are too threatening to his concepts. Two voters of different viewpoints are likely to have quite different perceptions of the same events, but neither is likely to be aware that his perceptions have been modified to match his prior beliefs about political reality.

When a significant part of the citizenry shares a basic set of beliefs about the political system, differences caused by personal backgrounds and diverse subcultural political environments are likely to cause very little misunderstanding or conflict. In a more pluralistic society, it may not even be possible for most of the voters to agree about the nature of the issue on which they are voting. After a candidate has been elected, his supporters may be quite upset to discover that they disagree sharply among themselves about the nature of the policies that he has promised to carry out.

Although much of the process of formation of attitudes and opinion is not accessible to the rational conscious mind, a person can make rational and conscious changes in his belief structure. A person who has learned from his subcultural background to distrust change might later come to favor radical change as a result of the study of political and economic theory. Or someone from a radical background might be converted to conservatism. However, such conscious and logical decisions in most cases play a less important role than the subtler socializing influences.

The more a person's lifestyle involves day-to-day interaction with the government, the more likely it is that he will vote. Thus, there is a higher voter turnout in cities than in rural areas. Persons at the peak of their career activities turn out in proportionately larger numbers than either the elderly or the young. A greater proportion of the rich will vote than of the poor. To some extent, these contrasts simply reflect differing degrees of exposure to the socializing agencies of the polity. For example, people with a higher level of education tend to vote in greater numbers than do those with less formal education.

Many factors intertwine to create the impetus to vote and to participate in the legitimate political life of society. If the influences of affiliations such as religion and profession all point in the same direction, their influence on the voter tends to be cumulative. In all areas of his life, he is reinforced for the same attitudes toward voting. However, if these diverse influences cross-pressure the individual—that is, pull him in opposite directions either in terms of voting or abstaining or in terms of the way he casts his vote—then this individual becomes less likely to participate in the electoral process or to adhere to a clear pattern of behavior if he does participate. Such vacillation among various behavior patterns might account for the so-called independent voter, who frequently changes his voting patterns.

As the values of the society change, so may the patterns of behavior of its citizens. We might expect certain changes in voting patterns, corresponding to changes that are occurring in our society. At present, a man is more likely to vote than is a woman, and a white is more likely to vote than is a black. As these groups resocialize and come to view themselves as more active participants in the political culture, we might expect both women and blacks to become more active voters. Similarly, changes in values may produce changes in present patterns of affiliation with political parties, with candidates, and with political issues. Even the influence of the mass media on voter's choices may be overrated, because the vast amount of information given daily to a citizen is filtered through his individual perceptual grid system. For the most part, the media can influence the voters only to the extent that they can change the value systems and political beliefs of individual citizens. In producing such value changes, the media are acting as socializing agents, along with parents, peers, and other groups or individuals. The value system of any individual is produced by a combination of many socializing influences, and this value system in turn determines what he perceives of the political situation and how he reacts to these perceptions. The political activities of the citizens then affect the structure of the system and the political culture, and so feed back to modify the socializing influences. If the political system is to survive, this continuous feedback cycle must keep the value systems of its members in adequate correspondence with changing conditions. Because childhood influences play such a major role in socialization, the cycle is not very effective in producing rapid value changes to enable the system to adapt to rapid cultural or environmental changes.

If someone grows up in a subculture whose values are not overly divergent from those prevailing in the society as a whole, he will enter the political marketplace with a sense of security and will offer his vote and political support in return for expected benefits. Only if ambivalence created by contradictory belief systems becomes overwhelming will the person tend to avoid participation and to be uncertain about what he can expect from the political system. Such a cross-pressured person may not only decrease his participation in accepted political marketplaces such as election campaigns, but he may also seek involvement in other subsystems that seem to offer more certain benefits in return for his investment of time, effort, and commitment.

The extent to which both the active voter and the apathetic nonvoter find satisfaction in their respective modes of behavior will influence their future patterns of activity, as well as their future expectations and choices. The degree of frustration they feel will similarly influence both attitudes and behavior and will add to the storehouse of personal and collective experiences that shapes the values and assumptions of future generations. Thus, voting behavior provides a useful example of how a government can change in response to public demands, yet can remain stable by providing a structured marketplace where citizens can bargain for policies that meet their expectations. The success of the system in responding to changing demands reinforces support for the government and participation in political activities among the citizenry.

In these first two chapters, we have emphasized the psychological variables said to be related to political participation. In Part Two we shall focus on the organizational, legal, and institutional factors related to participation, and on the role played by organizations in facilitating individual and group participation. We shall be looking in greater detail at the costs and profits associated with a person's decision to participate in the political marketplace.

SUMMARY

Certain trends and patterns emerge from an analysis of political behavior over time and across cultural boundaries. Political science as a disciplined field of inquiry seeks to abstract from these complex observations a general explanation of the interactions between citizens and the governmental structure of their society.

The analogy of the marketplace provides a useful general model for descriptions of the continuous interactions between individuals and the political structures that govern their society. In the political marketplace, individuals and groups organized around common interests meet to bargain with one another and to express their demands to the decisionmakers of the society. The government establishes regulations for the conduct of the marketplace and administers punishment to those who violate its regulations. All of the various transactions between parts of the citizenry or between citizens and the government can be viewed as bargaining exchanges in which each party offers to give something of value in return for certain benefits. The results of this give and take will never fully satisfy every individual, but when functioning properly the marketplace will produce results that keep most members of the society reasonably content with the situation. Because the marketplace does a reasonable job of meeting their demands, the citizens will grant legitimacy to the government and its regulations, even when they disagree with some particular decision.

As long as the behavior of supporting the government is rewarded by adequate benefits for a significant proportion of the population, the pattern of systemic behavior will be reinforced, the values of the political culture will be strengthened, and the system itself will remain intact. However, there will almost certainly be some individuals or groups who are frustrated and angry because they feel that they have not been rewarded fairly for their investment in supporting the system. Asystemic subcultures are likely to form, carrying on the necessary interactions of daily life outside of the established political system. Members of an asystemic subculture regard the government as irrelevant to their lives, and they cease to identify with the values of the general political culture. Living by their own rules, they are likely sooner or later to violate important governmental regulations, and to feel that they have been treated unjustly when the government imposes sanctions upon them. They may then view the government as a hindrance to their subculture and may turn to antisystemic activities.

Antisystemic groups can also arise directly if citizens within the political culture feel that they have been treated unjustly by the government. If a person feels that he has not been fairly rewarded for playing by the rules, he may cease to view the government as legitimate. If enough members of the society view the government as illegitimate and refuse to obey its regulations, the political marketplace may cease to function effectively. The stage is then set for a political revolution—a drastic change in the political system brought about by activities that the old system did not recognize as proper forms of political action.

A person's behavior in the political marketplace is determined by his set of values and beliefs, which in turn were formed through the process of socialization by influences from parents, peers, school, church, and the experiences of his own life. These values and beliefs act as a filter through which he perceives the political situation, and they determine the attitudes and actions that he will regard as appropriate to the perceived situation. In a pluralistic society, many people are likely to be cross-pressured by conflicting socializing influences; such people are unsure about what to expect from the political marketplace, and they may become alienated from the political system. A set of values and beliefs shared by a large group of individuals can be called an ideology. Cultural misperception is likely to arise when bargaining occurs between individuals or groups with differing values or ideologies.

Our model of the political marketplace assumes that individuals and groups try to make rational choices, maximizing their profits and minimizing their costs in each interaction. However, we also recognize the extreme importance of such factors as values and perceptions in understanding the choices that are made. In effect, our task as political scientists often becomes that of seeking to discover why a given choice appeared rational to those who made it.

We turn next to an analysis of political exchange within the United States and within some other national political systems.

REFERENCES

Campbell, Angus, Philip E. Converse, Warren E. Miller, and Donald E. Stokes. *The American Voter.* New York: Wiley, 1964.

Easton, David. *A Systems Analysis of Political Life.* New York: Wiley, 1965.

Lipset, Seymour Martin. *Political Man.* Garden City, N.J.: Doubleday, 1960.

Tullock, Gordon. *Private Wants, Public Needs.* New York: Basic Books, 1970.

National Exchange

PART II

Chapter 3 explores political exchange within the nation-state, using the United States as an example. Chapter 4 compares this example with processes of exchange in other nation-states. In these chapters, we attempt to reveal the unity of the political process beneath the peculiarities of history and culture that make individual nations seem quite different. We use the model of exchange in the political marketplace to demonstrate common features of the political process among diverse nations. The model also helps us explore the nature of the differences that do exist among nations with dissimilar histories, political structures, and practices. Of particular importance for an understanding of current events is our examination of the dynamics of political change in the Third World. We find that modernization is a worldwide phenomenon, with similar causes and consequences through many different cultures.

Political Exchange in the United States

CHAPTER 3

INSTITUTIONS AND POLICY FORMATION

In the political marketplace, the political leader acts as an entre-preneur. He asks citizens to invest political resources (such as money and organized political activity) in his campaign. In return, he promises both tangible and psychological rewards to those who have sup-ported him. If he succeeds in gaining office, he can use his authority to make decisions that will benefit his constituents in a variety of ways. He can provide tangible benefits both through favorable rulings on exchanges directly involving his supporters and through favorable decisions on more general matters of public policy.

For the purposes of this discussion, we define public policy as the set of authoritative decisions made by the government about

1. the rules and regulations under which individuals and groups may carry on bargaining in the political marketplace;

2. the nature, quantity, and distribution of public goods and services; and

3. the amount and distribution of tax levies upon the citizenry to pay for the public goods and services.

The public goods and services include national defense, education, health and welfare services, the social security system, highways, and a wide variety of government-funded jobs. For each of these areas, contracts worth millions of dollars must be awarded to various groups and individuals. The successful political leader may be able to reward his supporters with such contracts, with government positions in the administration of programs, and with the appointment of sympathetic administrators—as well as with favorable distributions of the taxes and of the benefits themselves.

In addition to these tangible rewards, the political leader may offer various kinds of psychological rewards to those who support him. Citizens may gain satisfaction simply from supporting an individual they admire or a cause they regard as just. They may attempt to improve their status within the community through association with the leaders of the political campaign, or later through positions of power or influence in the government.

On the other side of the bargain, the political leader also obtains both tangible and psychological rewards through his exchange with his constituents. Tangible rewards for the leader include salaries and other financial benefits, as well as the opportunity to exercise authority in ways that will benefit his own interests. Sometimes he may be able to obtain kickbacks or other benefits not recognized by the legal structure of the political marketplace. The leader obtains psychological rewards to the extent that the act of leadership satisfies his basic personality needs.

Philosophers have long debated the ideal balance to be struck in the bargain between the citizenry and the leader. Obviously, an ideal leader should always seek to make decisions that will be best for the general welfare of the society. A leader who has obtained his position primarily in order to garner tangible rewards (legal or extralegal) is apt to put his own financial interests ahead of the general welfare. On the other hand, a leader who seeks mainly to satisfy his own need for a position of leadership may well place his retention of the position above the general welfare. Plato tried to solve this dilemma by suggesting the philosopher–king as the ideal leader. From childhood, this leader would be deprived of personal property or a private family. All of his needs would be supplied by the community; in return, he would be forced to undergo a lifetime of rigorous training in temperance, courage, and wisdom. Perhaps such a philosopher–king would indeed serve the general welfare without thoughts of personal gain, but the political culture of the United States has established quite a different system for training and choosing its leaders.

Any American citizen can choose to seek a position of political leadership. He enters the political marketplace to seek support from other citizens, offering various benefits in return. Each citizen weighs the benefits promised by a particular leader against the cost of money, time, and effort to be invested in his support. The leader also computes his own profit from the bargain, balancing his expected benefits against the costs in money, time, energy, and political status to be expended in obtaining those benefits.

The Presidency

In terms of the political marketplace, the American presidency is the highest reward a political entrepreneur can hope to gain in the United States. A political leader who attains the presidency has successfully and efficiently employed scarce political resources. He has invested time, money, effort, and organization to produce a winning coalition of sectors—political support sufficient to obtain a majority of votes in the electoral college. In return, the President must use his authority to reward those groups and individuals that invested their resources in his campaign.

The President plays an important role in establishing public policy, both through his own decisions and through his influence upon public opinion and upon other political leaders. His power to appoint individuals to various government positions is extremely important. Interest groups offer political support in return for the appointment of friendly administrators to whom they have access. Farm groups hope to obtain a Secretary of Agriculture who will favor price supports or high farm incomes; cattle raisers seek a Secretary of the Interior who will permit grazing of herds on public lands at nominal fees. Individuals may supply important political support in return for a prestigious appointment as an ambassador or presidential assistant. Other important presidential powers include the proposal of policy initiatives in the State of the Union Address and in televised press conferences or speeches, the development of the federal budget with the help of the Office of Management and Budget, the use of various political favors or threats to create congressional coalitions that will support various legislative programs, and the opportunity as chief administrator to oversee the functioning of all old and new policies and to establish priorities among them.

The Constitution describes a system of checks and balances, in which power is distributed fairly equally among the legislative, executive, and judicial branches of the government. The people are represented most directly in the Congress, which has the power to make the laws, set taxes, and order government expenditures. Even here, the Senate (originally elected indirectly through state legislatures) was intended as a group of older, better educated, wiser people of longer government experience, who would act as a check upon the more directly chosen House of Representatives. The judicial branch is visualized as a group of people deliberately removed from political pressures who can act with impartiality and wisdom in settling disputes that arise under the laws and in applying the laws fairly to individual cases. The powers of the presidency are not very fully described in the Constitution, partly because there was extensive disagreement among the framers about the proper extent of those powers. The President is made commander-in-chief of the armed forces, he is empowered to represent the United States in dealings with other nations (though the Senate must approve his commitments), and he is put in charge of a vaguely described executive department that will carry out the laws passed by Congress. He can veto acts of Congress (but a two-thirds majority of each house can override his veto), and he is required occasionally to report to Congress on the state of the nation and to recommend new legislation.

The actual powers of the modern presidency have evolved through two centuries of experience under the Constitution. Overall, the President has become a much more powerful leader than the constitutional description implies, but the power of the president has varied greatly through the history of our nation. For example, Abraham Lincoln exercised extreme power during the Civil War, but the power of the presidency was greatly overshadowed by that of Congress through the last quarter of the nineteenth century. Theodore Roosevelt, Woodrow Wilson, and Franklin D. Roosevelt each extended the powers of the presidency, while the intervening presidents were relatively weak in comparison to Congress. During the presidency of John Kennedy, many political scholars began to call for a return to a strong presidency, arguing that Congress was unable to meet the needs of an age of rapid change. Presidents Johnson and Nixon greatly enhanced the powers of the presidency in both foreign and domestic affairs. The events leading to the resignation of President Nixon caused a general reassessment of the advantages and disadvantages of a strong president. In the wake of Watergate and Vietnam, many political scholars (including most of those who had been advocating a stronger presidency a decade before) have begun to call for more stringent limitations on presidential power.

The expansion of presidential power over the two centuries since the Constitution was written has come about chiefly in two ways. First, Congress has delegated authority to the president, particularly through the creation of executive departments given extensive authority to carry out various complex policies under presidential direction—but also through acquiescence in various cases where presidents have exercised new powers that later became traditional. Most such expansions of presidential power have occurred during crises—economic dislocations or depressions, or national emergencies due to war or threat of war—when decisive and rapid action was needed, but Congress was unable to reach swift agreement on the action to be taken. In such situations, the political leaders in Congress often were willing to let the president assume the political risks involved in making authoritative decisions that might not prove popular with the citizenry. After the crisis has passed, the expanded presidential powers have usually remained in the legal structure, although some individual presidents have not chosen (or been able) to exercise them fully.

The second major source of new presidential powers has been a popular demand for swift and decisive decision-making during times of crisis, coupled with a willingness on the part of the citizenry to trust particularly compelling individual presidents to extricate the nation from crises. This popular support for strong presidential action has usually triggered or supported the tendency for Congress to delegate authority to the president in times of crisis.

A closer look at the political situation surrounding the resignation of President Nixon will help to illustrate the practical limits on presidential power and the nature of the political bargaining in which the president is involved. Although the Constitution provides the mechanism of impeachment for removal of a president who has proved incompetent or extreme in the exercise of his authority, this mechanism has rarely been used. The unusual situation of a serious attempt to impeach a president provides an illuminating example of the kinds of political exchange that occur in less extreme form in normal political bargaining.

Richard Nixon was first elected president in 1968, winning a very narrow victory over Hubert Humphrey. In that election, Nixon received 43.4 percent of the popular vote, Humphrey 42.7 percent, and George Wallace (candidate of the extremely conservative American Independent Party) 13.5 percent. Nixon's success was in large part due to the political support he had accumulated during the preceding four years, when he worked for various Republican candidates around the country. He was also helped by a popular rejection of the Vietnam War (which Humphrey had stoutly defended as Lyndon Johnson's vice president) and by the fact that Wallace attracted the votes of many groups that had traditionally supported Democratic candidates.

Nixon's success in using presidential powers to attract political support is shown by the results of the 1972 election, when Nixon received 60.7 percent of the popular vote, while George McGovern received only 37.5 percent. Of course, Nixon's showing in this election was somewhat enhanced by a widespread distrust of McGovern that led many persons opposed to Nixon to avoid voting altogether. Only about 56 percent of the voting-age population cast votes in 1972, compared to about 61 percent in 1968. Nonetheless, the results of the 1972 election show that Nixon did have strong political support from the citizenry at that time, even though the burglars arrested in Democratic headquarters at the Watergate in June had already been linked to Nixon's campaign committee.

Soon after the 1972 election, Nixon's political support began to erode in the wake of a flood of disclosures about the Watergate scandal. By July 1973, enough facts were known to lead to an investigation by a special Senate committee. During these hearings, Nixon was accused of taking an active part in a conspiracy to "cover up" White House involvement in the original Watergate break-in and other illegal political acts. The existence of a taping system in the White House was revealed, and investigators demanded access to the tapes in order to determine Nixon's role in the alleged coverup. In October, Nixon fired the special prosecutor appointed to handle the Watergate case because the prosecutor had insisted upon access to the tapes. Both the Attorney General and his deputy resigned in protest against Nixon's action, and angry and alarmed citizens flooded Washington with letters, postcards, and telegrams demanding congressional action.

In April 1974, Nixon did make public transcripts of some tapes. The transcripts themselves were somewhat damaging to his claims of innocence; even more damaging was the evidence that he had released only the least incriminating portions of various conversations. By this time, Nixon's political support had weakened to such an extent that a serious move toward impeachment proceedings was underway in the House of Representatives. In July, the Supreme Court ruled that Nixon was required to release more tapes, and formal impeachment hearings began in the House Judiciary Committee.

On August 4, the House Judiciary Committee voted to recommend impeachment. The next day, Nixon released some more tapes, which showed that he had ordered a "coverup" within the first week after the arrests at the Watergate. On August 6, Nixon announced his intention to remain in office and to defend himself against the impeachment charges in the House and Senate. However, it soon became clear that most political leaders were no longer willing to support him, and on August 8 Nixon announced that he would resign on the following day—the first presidential resignation in United States history.

Under normal conditions, "presidential politics" involves the need for political support from two groups: (1) the general voting population, and (2) other political leaders. In order to be elected and reelected, a president must have sufficient popular support to obtain a majority of votes in the electoral college. In order to function effectively between elections, the president must have sufficient support from Congress and from other political leaders to enable him to carry out the policies that he has promised to his supporters.

As soon as it became clear that formal impeachment proceedings would be brought against Nixon, he faced an unusual political situation that called for an approach which has been dubbed "impeachment politics." Nixon's ability to remain in office would depend upon his ability to convince at least 34 senators to vote against his conviction in the Senate trial—or to obtain support from a majority of those who would have to approve the impeachment charges in the House Judiciary Committee and the full House before the trial could begin. The effort to obtain this crucial political support against impeachment led Nixon to make dramatic changes in his positions on many political issues. This episode of "impeachment politics" therefore provides an unusually vivid illustration of political bargaining.

During the exposure of the Watergate scandal, the Nixon administration backed away from its earlier proposals for a Family

Assistance Program (a centralized national welfare plan) and a comprehensive system of national health insurance. The president stopped supporting these proposals in an attempt to keep the support of more conservative Republicans and southern Democrats in the Senate, who were opposed to these seemingly liberal reforms. Removal of active administration support for these two programs was essentially an implicit trade for the much-needed support of conservative political leaders in the impeachment struggle. The original proposal of the programs had been a bid for political support from those large groups in the population who would benefit from such programs. However, liberal political leaders who would favor such programs were already firmly committed to Nixon's impeachment on grounds that he had abused the powers of the presidency and obstructed justice. Therefore, "impeachment politics" required that Nixon risk the loss of public support in order to maintain a core of conservative support in the Senate.

Other examples of Nixon's attempts to win conservative support can be cited. In June 1974, the administration withdrew its support of a land-use bill and allowed its defeat in the Senate, thus rewarding conservatives who had strongly opposed the bill. Similarly, the administration ceased to make strong efforts to reach accord with the Soviet Union in the second phase of the Strategic Arms Limitation Talks (SALT). Those leaders in the Senate who distrusted détente with the Soviet Union and opposed the SALT agreements were the same individuals whose support Nixon needed to prevent his impeachment.

In the pre-Watergate political marketplace, Nixon had been offering various benefits to obtain wide public support for his administration. Such support would both assist the next Republican candidate for the presidency and help to ensure a favorable place for Nixon in the history of the nation. When the threat of impeachment became serious, Nixon turned instead to political bargaining that would obtain the support of a minority of staunch conservatives in the Senate. The conservatives in turn were able to use their potential vote in an impeachment trial as a strong bargaining lever in their attempts to obtain Nixon's support for their policy positions.

When Nixon resigned in August 1974, Vice President Gerald Ford became president. Ford had become Vice President in December 1973, replacing Spiro Agnew who had resigned in October with the admission that he had evaded income tax on kickbacks he had received during his governorship of Maryland. Ford had been nominated by Nixon and confirmed by Congress in the first use of procedures set up by the Twenty-Fifth Amendment to the Constitution (ratified in 1967). Although Ford had been elected to Congress by the population of Michigan's Fifth Congressional District and chosen House Minority Leader by Republican Congressmen, he had never been a candidate in a national election. Because he had not established a base of political support among the national population, he entered the presidency with very little political capital. He could not offer his influence over a majority of the nation's voters in return for political benefits from other leaders. In fact, he was himself in the position of having to use his authority to repay Nixon and the Congress for having made him President. Polls did show general popular support for Ford when he took office. Voters who have invested money, time, or effort in a candidate are likely to continue to support him for some time, even if they are not pleased with some of his decisions after he achieves office. The weakness of Ford's popular support has been shown by the extreme fluctuations in his poll ratings from month to month.

Because Ford has little political capital to offer in bargaining, he has not been able to obtain support from Congress for his policies. In many cases, Congress has mustered a two-thirds majority to override his vetoes (as in the case of a December 1974 bill to extend veteran's benefits). Congress has often ignored his requests for legislative action on his economic proposals, although at this writing (mid-1975) it has not been very successful in formulating its own policies. Ford's political weakness is due both to his unique position as a nonelected president and to the overwhelming defeat of Republican candidates in the 1974 congressional elections (apparently largely a reaction against the scandals of the Nixon administration).

Political capital is the reservoir of support that a president gains through exchanges during the campaign with political sectors, party factions, and the electorate. He obtains commitments of support in return for his promises of certain actions after his election. In turn, he then can use this political capital after his election by offering his influence in political bargaining with other leaders to get his policies carried out. If he is successful in this bargaining, he obtains additional public support because his policies do provide benefits for various individuals and groups.

Having entered the presidency without much political capital, President Ford is unable to carry out an effective policy that might increase his stock of political capital. His only hope for breaking this vicious circle is to take some well-publicized action that does not require much support from other political leaders, in hopes of winning significant and committed public support. His dramatic action in ordering the armed rescue of the crew of the *Mayaguez* (an action taken on his own authority as President without the need for congressional support) could be viewed as such an action.

We have applied our model of exchange in the political marketplace to a discussion of Nixon's threatened impeachment and of Ford's first year in the presidency. The model does prove useful in understanding the political situation under these very unusual circumstances. Throughout this book we shall find the model useful as well in understanding more normal political processes, but we shall also find it useful to return to these unique political crises because they expose certain features of the political process in unusual clarity.

Before leaving this topic, we should take one final look at Nixon's resignation. We have discussed his reliance upon support from the right wing of both parties to avoid impeachment as his general support declined in the face of increasing revelations of scandal. We have seen how he offered various bargains in order to maintain that conservative support (Figure 1). Yet, when the actual impeachment crisis arrived, the conservative support evaporated. Nixon announced his resignation after prominent conservative leaders from Congress met privately to inform him that they would not vote for him in the impeachment proceedings. Why did his efforts to use "impeachment politics" fail?

In part, Nixon finally lost support because many of the conservatives on whom he had relied were people who placed a high value upon moral conduct; many of these people were genuinely shocked by the language and conduct revealed when Nixon was finally forced to release many of the tapes of his White House conversations. Even more important, however, was the fact that Nixon's political capital had dwindled to the point that he had little with which to bargain. As he lost popular support (both through revelations of scandal and through his deliberate policy changes aimed at winning conservative support in the Senate), he lost political influence that he could offer in exchange for support from political leaders. As more and more leaders added their power to the forces seeking his impeachment, those forces themselves became able to offer ever better bargains for the support of the conservatives. By August 5 it had become clear

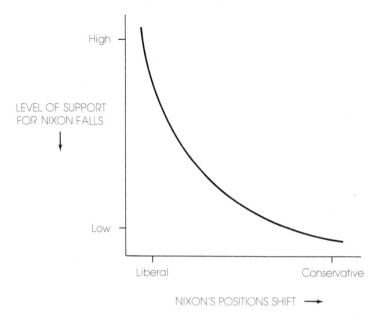

Figure 1
As his impeachment loomed and his popular support fell away, Nixon
abandoned social reforms in a bid to retain the support of conservatives.

that the conservatives had much more to lose by supporting Nixon than
they had to gain. Therefore, they began to use their political capital to bargain with Ford, rather than risking that capital to save Nixon
from impeachment when it seemed clear that, even if he remained
President, Nixon would have so little political capital left that he would
be unable to offer any further benefits to the conservatives.

The political bargaining that goes on in normal "presidential
politics" is perhaps more complex and certainly less visible than
these extreme examples we have discussed. The political marketplace is complex; it involves a constantly shifting network of agreements—both explicit and implicit—among individuals and a
wide variety of groups, many of which are overlapping or themselves shifting. Although the details of this bargaining are often difficult
to determine precisely, the general patterns can be discerned. Skill
at handling this complex political bargaining process seems to be a
major requirement for success as a presidential candidate and as a
president.

Congress

Like all organizations, legislative bodies offer tangible and intangible rewards to their members, including power and prestige as well as more idiosyncratic benefits. Within the Congress itself, members are rewarded for behaving in a manner that is adjudged desirable by tradition and by the legislative leaders. Such patterns of behavior are prescribed by formal rules and reinforced by informal norms. By longstanding tradition, for example, members of the majority party with the greatest seniority (length of service) are given their choice of committee chairmanships, but this tradition is occasionally overruled when a particular member has behaved in a manner that his colleagues regard as unacceptable. Other customs of the legislative marketplace that facilitate day-to-day interactions among members include courtesy, reciprocity (the exchange of favors), and specialization (the development of expertise in a specific area of legislation).

Legislators who conform to congressional rules and customs are rewarded, not only with prestige and acceptance, but also with an enhanced capacity to achieve policy goals that they and their constituents value. Those who fail to conform are either deprived of these rewards or suffer sanctions that increase their costs in future transactions within the legislative marketplace. A few examples from recent history will illustrate this process. From 1950 through 1954, Senator Joseph McCarthy played a prominent role in American politics with his charges and investigations of Communist infiltration of the U.S. government. A series of extreme charges against the Army and its leaders in 1954 led many senators to conclude that McCarthy had exceeded the bounds of reasonable behavior. The Senate voted (67 to 22) to censure McCarthy for misconduct. Although McCarthy retained his formal position in the Senate (committee assignments, for example), his charges and opinions were thereafter treated with little respect by other senators and were given little attention by the press.

Senator Thomas Dodd was another politician who gained prominence by attacking Communist influences within the U.S. Like McCarthy, Dodd annoyed other senators by overstepping the bounds of accepted courtesy in his charges. Nonetheless, when two members of Dodd's staff made public charges that he had diverted campaign funds to his own personal use, most senators at first tended to defend their fellow-member against these charges by non-members of the Senate. However, Dodd asked for an investigation, and the Senate Ethics Committee reported that he had indeed made personal use of some $160,000 in campaign funds and had engaged in other unethical practices to his own financial benefit. The Senate in 1967 voted (92 to 5) to censure him for the misuse of campaign funds. Again, the censure was the only formal punishment, but it was accompanied by a loss of prestige and acceptance that left Dodd with little real influence in the Senate. In the 1970 election, voters refused to return him to his Senate seat.

The case of Congressman Adam Clayton Powell involved a complex range of issues. Since his Harlem district had first elected him to Congress in 1944, Powell had gloried in his dual image as a spokesman for blacks and as a playboy, and his constituents apparently loved him for it. By the mid-1960s, Powell was attracting national attention for his extravagant living. He spent much of his time vacationing in tropical tourist spots, always billing his expenses to the government, posing for press photographs with various beautiful women who accompanied him. His wife (who lived in Puerto Rico) drew a $20,000 salary as part of his office staff. Powell seldom tried to conceal his behavior, and he often defended it by claiming that other members of Congress did the same things in secrecy. Other congressmen were quite upset about his behavior, at least in part because Powell was publicly carrying to ridiculous extremes the privileges that they enjoyed more discreetly. Although many blacks regarded Powell as a hero for his open defiance of the Establishment standards, other congressmen were under heavy pressure from their white constituents to do something about Powell's excesses. In 1967, the Democrats broke with tradition to deny Powell the committee chairmanship to which his seniority entitled him. The full House then voted (365 to 65) to deny him his seat on grounds of flagrant misconduct, declaring the seat vacant and ordering a special election to fill it. The Harlem district responsed by reelecting Powell, and the Supreme Court later ruled that the House had acted unconstitutionally in expelling him. However, the Democratic caucus continued to deny Powell any privileges based on his seniority and much of his influence in the House was lost. In the 1970 elections, his district failed to return him to Congress.

These examples illustrate the importance of a congressman's standing within the legislative body itself. If he loses his political bargaining power in the legislative markeplace, he can no longer produce the benefits for his constituents that will lead them to reelect him.

A legislator must value the rewards of a political career highly in order to risk the initial investment needed to gain a seat in the House or Senate. Other lucrative positions in business and government are available to most individuals who choose to become legislators. The decision to enter a campaign involves balancing the rewards of success against the costs of the campaign and of service as a legislator, taking into account the estimated chances of winning the election. In 1968, Governor Harold Hughes of Iowa decided to run for the Senate and won a very narrow election victory. After serving one term in the Senate, Hughes chose not to run for reelection in 1974. Apparently Hughes decided that the chance of winning reelection and the benefits to be obtained no longer outweighed the risks and costs. Perhaps he found that the return on his investment of time, energy, and money during his first term was insufficient, that he no longer valued the rewards of Senate service, or that he could gain greater benefits for the same cost in some other field of activity.

The U.S. Congress exhibits many of the features of a free marketplace. It is decentralized and is characterized by a relatively wide dispersal of power and influence. In order to comprehend its dynamics, we must analyze the role of the political parties and congressional committees that are the major internal structures of the congressional marketplace.

At the opening of each new Congress, the Democratic and Republican party members of each house meet in separate caucuses to choose their own leaders. These elections are exchanges within the party between coalitions of individuals; leadership positions are the rewards, and added workloads are the costs. The most important positions determined in these elections are those of majority and minority leaders in each house; in the House of Representatives, the majority-party caucus also chooses the Speaker of the House.

The primary function of the party leaders is to facilitate the work of Congress by scheduling debate and voting. Leaders also attempt to build coalitions to support or oppose specific pieces of legislation. In the latter capacity, leaders enter into exchanges with their colleagues as they bargain for votes. The bargaining advantages of the leader (such as potential rewards and deprivations at his disposal) are greater in the House than in the Senate because the House is a larger body and therefore has a greater need for centralization and rules conducive to efficient operation. Party loyalty—the feeling of acceptance among others with whom a member identifies—is one of the most important rewards that leaders trade for votes and compliance.

Congressional power is decentralized chiefly because of the committee system; here the political marketplace comes alive. In committees the demands made by various political sectors (organized labor, business, farmers, consumer groups, and so on) for public resources and policies are processed. Important political exchanges occur among the committee members, congressional leaders, and agents of the administration as they endeavor to negotiate legislation that will be approved by a majority of the committee members and then by majorities in the full House and Senate. Often the voting on the floor is no more than a formal ratification of a bargain already worked out in committee proceedings.

Attempts to produce legislation to deal with the problems of the energy crisis in 1974 provide a graphic illustration of the bargaining process. When the oil-producing nations drastically increased oil prices, leaders in the United States were made painfully aware of American dependence upon outside energy sources and of the fact that this dependence has been increasing for many years. There was an urgent call for new legislation that would ease the immediate impact of the increased oil prices and that would begin preparations for the development of new energy sources. A subcommittee chaired by Senator Henry Jackson (a Democrat from Washington) began hearings aimed at the eventual passage of an energy bill. In these hearings, various groups made their demands known. Representatives from the oil industry argued for policies and laws favorable to their interests. Consumer groups, such as homeowners who use heating oil and truck drivers, sought to influence the distribution of costs and benefits in other directions. Various demands were made about policy changes in regard to windfall profits, oil prices, tax advantages of the oil industry, and federal programs for energy research.

Consumer groups argued that the oil companies were making excessive profits from the energy crisis; they demanded that prices be rolled back and tax loopholes for the oil companies be closed. The political bargaining power of these consumer groups was enhanced by the fact that Senators feared a revolt by voters against high taxes and a slumping economy. Of course, the various consumer groups were not in complete harmony. Homeowners insisted that the price of heating oil must be kept low while any price increases were absorbed in the price of gasoline; truckdrivers insisted that the health of the economy depended upon a rollback in the cost of gasoline. Spokesmen for the oil industry insisted that high profits were needed to attract the capital needed to expand oil production and to develop alternative energy sources. They opposed any attempt to increase the costs of the oil corporations, and in fact called for additional tax benefits and federal grants to support research.

The bargaining was complicated still further by the arguments of environmentalists, who argued that the use of oil should be discouraged and that programs should be designed to halt the growth in energy use rather than to supply expanded supplies of energy. Furthermore, they opposed the strip mining of coal and the building of nuclear-powered generating plants, two of the major alternative energy sources that the energy corporations wanted to exploit. Spokesmen for the Ford administration argued for their own set of suggested policies, designed to benefit those whose political support the president was courting. Each senator argued for a set of policies that would best satisfy his own constituents.

This congressional marketplace provides a forum where such complex bargains can be hammered out. However, the process is seldom a rapid one. At this writing, after more than a year of bargaining, no complete public policy on energy has been developed. Congress has voted funds for energy research, but further bargaining is still needed to produce agreements on other aspects of energy policy.

While Senator Jackson's subcommittee was bargaining about energy policy, hundreds of other matters of public policy were being debated in other committees and subcommittees. A great number of groups made their demands known to the legislators on those matters that concerned them. These groups ranged from the National Rifle Association, the United Automobile Workers, and the National Association of Manufacturers to the Sierra Club, the National Educational Association, and Common Cause. Each organization used its political resources to bargain for policies desired by its members— and to influence general public opinion in its favor. The basic political resources of an organization are the votes of its members, the money or other resources that it can provide for political campaigns, and its ability to influence public opinion because of its status within the society.

It is quite useful to think of Congress as a political marketplace in which diverse interest groups seek scarce public resources (in the form of public policies and programs) and offer their political resources in return. Scarcity of public resources inevitably produces disputes; Congress provides a forum where these conflicts may be resolved. The various laws, programs, and policies sought by diverse groups determine the costs and rewards for the entire society. Groups particularly affected by some proposed policy, in turn, attempt to influence the allocation of costs and benefits in their own favor. In the legislative marketplace, these groups bargain indirectly through the various resources that each can offer in return for a desired vote by a legislator. They may also bargain directly as they make agreements to trade support for each other's positions on various issues.

Congress functions as a free marketplace because it is decentralized and pluralistic. No individual or group maintains absolute power or influence over the decision-making process. Party leaders have some power through their ability to allocate rewards within the structure of Congress, buth they must compete with the rewards offered by committee chairmen and interest groups who also seek to influence the votes of legislators. With its numerous centers of influence, Congress is easily accessible to any group that seeks to influence policy decisions. Because the cost of access is low and the probability of at least partial success is relatively high, these groups find participation in the congressional marketplace to be rewarding in itself. The public is apt to grant legitimacy to the congressional system, not because each individual is always satisfied with decisions that are made, but because he does perceive the possibility of shaping policy and achieving goals at acceptable costs (Figure 2).

The Courts

At first glance, it might seem that the judicial system lies outside the bargaining of the political marketplace. Traditionally, the courts have seldom been regarded as political institutions. However, a broad definition of the functions of courts and laws and their relationship to public policy allows us to include them in the exchange analysis.

The judicial system makes decisions to settle disputes that arise under the laws and regulations—disputes among individuals, groups, and the government. The judicial system also defines the rights and obligations of individuals and groups under the laws and constitution. In the United States in particular, the judicial system interprets laws governing the rights and duties of citizens within society. The laws may be generally defined as authoritative regulations that establish a pattern of benefits and costs designed to encourage or discourage behavior judged desirable or undesirable by the political

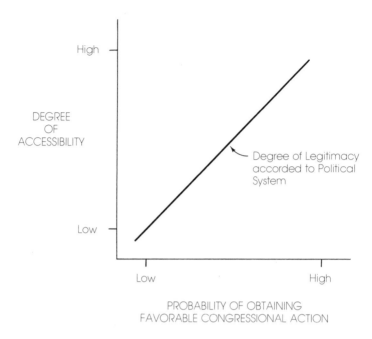

Figure 2

As various groups compete for favorable congressional actions, they perceive that their chances of success are linked to the accessibility of centers of influence in the Congress. The degree of legitimacy accorded to the political system is a function of accessibility and the probability of success.

system. The judicial system makes the decisions needed to apply the laws to particular cases; it also acts to resolve any contradictions that may arise among various laws or between laws and the constitution.

In the United States, both state and federal courts interpret the meaning of language used in laws; in doing so, they often attempt to determine the intentions of the legislators who proposed the laws or regulations in question. In fulfilling this role of interpretation, the courts in effect play a secondary policy-making role. In some cases, court decisions have significantly altered the terms of entry to the political marketplace and the distribution of costs and benefits among groups and individuals in the marketplace.

The issues of civil rights and liberties provide many examples of the role of the judicial system in determining policy. In 1896, the

Supreme Court interpreted the Constitution to mean that a state could provide separate public facilities for whites and for blacks, so long as the separate facilities were of essentially equal quality. In 1954, the Supreme Court reversed this ruling and declared that "separate educational facilities are inherently unequal" and therefore are forbidden by the Constitution. Over the following years, federal courts issued many decisions interpreting the Constitution and various laws in ways that significantly altered the terms of interactions between black and white Americans. The courts decided that the Constitution requires efforts to eliminate the economic, political, and social disadvantages long borne by black Americans.

White citizens who opposed integration of schools and other public facilities used a wide variety of legal and extralegal tactics to attempt the nullification of the effects of the court rulings. This opposition in turn roused many blacks and whites to use legal and extralegal tactics aimed at furthering the changes initiated by the courts. Greater numbers of black Americans decided to join political parties, to vote, to organize for political action, and in general to participate in the political marketplace. The increased competition among politicians for the growing political resources of the black voters soon led to the passage of civil rights laws aimed at further decreasing the disadvantages of black Americans.

The initial impetus for this significant change in the political marketplace came through court decisions. These decisions significantly eased the costs of entrance into the political marketplace for blacks and also led to significant changes in general public opinion about the issue. Decisions made in the legislative marketplace then began to shift in a new direction as the balances of bargaining power were changed. In other matters of public policy, the role of the courts in establishing policy may be less obvious, but it is often significant.

The structure of the judicial marketplace, however, is quite different from that of the legislative marketplace. The judges in federal courts are not subject to election and are forbidden to accept most kinds of benefits from groups and individuals; therefore, relatively few political resources can be brought to bear in bargaining to influence their decisions. Access to the judicial marketplace is severely limited; only groups and individuals with a legitimate interest in a case being decided are allowed to express their views, and even then the nature of their participation is strictly limited by rules of court procedure. On matters of federal law, the final decision is made by the nine justices of the Supreme Court, whose power to interpret the law and Constitution is for all practical purposes absolute. Because the judicial marketplace is neither decentralized nor pluralistic, it does not function as a free marketplace.

The structure of the judicial system regulates the costs of access to the marketplace. For example, questions about the rights of defendants in criminal cases can be regarded as questions about the costs that an individual must bear to gain a fair trial and the resources that he must invest to insure for himself qualified legal assistance. Only recently has the Supreme Court ruled that free legal counsel must be provided for indigent defendants accused of noncapital offenses (the right to counsel in capital cases had been established earlier). Recent decisions enlarging the rights of defendants—particularly those of low economic status—are largely responses to the growing awareness of the fact that the structure of the system favors the interests of the person or corporation of high economic status. A poor defendant may be forced to accept some punishment through plea bargaining; a rich defendant can pay for the legal counsel needed to fight a case through many appeals and perhaps eventually to win a favorable decision.

In the legislative marketplace, even an indigent citizen has at least his vote with which to exert some influence on the decision-making process. In the judicial marketplace, an individual's bargaining power has in the past been much more affected by his socioeconomic status. The current efforts to alter the structure of the marketplace may eventually lead to a more even set of costs for all citizens participating in the system. In part, these changes represent a response to shifting public opinion about the nature of justice and of the judicial system; in part, they represent an effort by judges to change public views and opinions. The closed structure of the judicial marketplace is intended to isolate judges from political pressures and permit them to make decisions based on impartial consideration of the laws, the facts in a case, and the general welfare of the society. In practice, this closed structure often makes it difficult for many individuals or groups to enter the marketplace on an equal footing with other individuals or groups. At present it is clear that a person's political and financial resources, his social status, and his ethnic affiliations do influence his success in bargaining for his own benefit within the judicial system. If justice is a public good, then like many public goods it is inadequately provided to those most in need of it.

LOCAL GOVERNMENT

Much of what we have said about the executive, legislative, and judicial institutions of national government holds true as well for state, county, and municipal governments. In order to further our understanding of subnational government in the United States, we will look here at the question of the proper scope and size of local government and at the nature of interactions between federal and local governments. We will use revenue sharing as an example of federal–local interaction.

Until recent times, cities and towns in the United States (with the exception of Washington, D.C.) have developed, grown, and died in a relatively unplanned fashion. Towns have tended to form at the mouths and forks of rivers, at natural ports, and at trading crossroads. In the western part of the country, many towns grew up along railroads and stage lines, where goods and people were transferred to and from a long-distance transportation system. The industrial revolution, migration, and population increase have created the great cities that exist today, but only in recent years has interest been renewed in the question of the proper size of a local city government. How large an area and how large a population should ideally be joined under a single local government? Another important question now receiving attention is that of which services can better be provided by local or state governments and which can better be provided by the national government. In the twentieth century, the national government has generally controlled more of the necessary resources than have local and state governments, and so the federal role has expanded into such areas as education, welfare, health, housing, pollution, and law enforcement—areas that had traditionally fallen largely under local or state governmental control.

Using concepts borrowed from the field of economics, we can discuss the relative merits of centralization versus decentralization of political power and the problem of the appropriate size of a governmental unit for performance of its role in the political system. We have established that the existence of government is a cost to every citizen and that any services provided by the government will ultimately be financed through taxation. The cost of government services will vary with the size of the government, the size of the population that it serves, and the extent to which the government must compete in the general market with individuals and groups for the services that it purchases. For any particular service that a government might provide, there will be some size of administrative unit that is optimal for the greatest efficiency in producing the necessary amount at the least cost to the citizenry. Unfortunately, it is seldom possible to predict this optimal size from theoretical considerations. Citizens must decide empirically whether the appropriate governmental unit to handle a given task should be formed by combining several small towns, by splitting a large city into a number of districts, by forming units composed of a number of counties or states, and so on—or by making use of some existing level of government.

Environmental issues provide good examples of this problem of size. Because the effects of any specific case of pollution are geographically limited, and because the extent to which a particular act causes serious pollution varies greatly from one locality to another, the regulation of pollution has largely been left to the local governments in the past. With increasing population density and increasing industrialization, however, problems of pollution have become matters of national concern. In some urban areas that include several cities or counties, regional governmental units have been established to regulate air pollution. Control of water pollution has in some cases required cooperative action by several states along a coastline or river. The national government has become involved in such matters as regulating the amount of pollution emitted by automobiles and sewage plants. Many individuals have become annoyed with the decisions made by these larger governmental units, feeling that they do not adequately allow for the peculiarities of local situations, which might call for either more or less stringent regulations than those issued for the larger area. It is very difficult to reach an objective evaluation of the proper governmental level on which each kind of pollution should be regulated.

Throughout the history of the United States, and particularly in the twentieth century, there has been a tendency for the national government to assume more and more of the functions formerly handled by local and state governments. In part, this trend toward increasing centralization is a result of improving communications and increasing mobility; citizens have become more aware of conditions in all parts of the country and are more apt to regard distant parts of the country as parts of their own society. In part also it is due to the efficiency of the income-tax system (with taxes withheld from the salaries of most individuals automatically) as a way of distributing

costs among the citizens. In recent decades, the trend has been accelerated because the national government has been dominated by
leaders who believe that a strong national government can provide
many goods and services more justly and evenly among the citizenry
than can the smaller governmental units. Very recently, however, there
has been an increasing feeling among the population that the
national government has grown so large as to be highly inefficient.
Services are not reaching the individuals who need them; a large
amount of the money obtained through taxation is being used to support an unwieldy, unresponsive and inefficient government
bureaucracy.

Revenue-sharing is in part a recognition of the economies to
be gained by maintaining a vital system of local governments, able
to cope efficiently with problems peculiar to each locality. In essence,
revenue-sharing is an exchange cycle among three participants.
The citizen pays taxes to the federal government, which uses part of
this revenue to cover its costs of operation and the costs of the
services it provides to the public. The national government then allo-
cates the remaining portion of its revenue to local and state governments. These subnational governments in turn are expected to
improve and expand the services that they offer to their constituents,
or to reduce the burden of local taxes imposed upon their citizens. The
expected benefit of the exchange for the national government is
freedom from responsibility for particular programs and expenditures
that have proven burdensome for one reason or another—often
because of demands for increased local control.

If revenue-sharing results mainly in benefits for the economically
and politically advantaged (because of tax reductions or the expansion of programs designed to benefit those already enjoying high
benefits from government), then the general citizenry will eventually
reject the program as unsatisfactory and unjust. In that event, new
demands will be voiced, calling for alterations in the distribution of
advantages through changes in the revenue-sharing program or
through greater federal oversight of local expenditures. On the
other hand, if revenue-sharing works as its designers hoped to increase
the efficiency of governmental services, there will be a general demand for further expansion and improvement of the revenue-sharing program. The experiences of all three participants in the bargain
—national government, local governments, and citizens—will be important in determining the nature of future bargains on the matter.

BUREAUCRACY

Bureaucracy is a ubiquitous feature of any modern or modernizing society in this last quarter of the twentieth century. There are many ways to describe and analyze bureaucracy, leading to many negative and positive judgments about it. Here we limit ourselves to a discussion of a few of its relevant characteristics. Public bureaucracy extracts resources such as taxes from the society in general and supplies services to the general society in return, carrying out the public policy approved by the political leadership. The bureaucracy itself consumes many goods and services. For example, many war materials are purchased only by government agencies; the welfare of these agencies then becomes a major factor in the welfare (and economic survival) of industries that supply the war materials. In many bargaining situations, the leaders of the government agency and the leaders of the industries that work with it act together because their interests coincide. Often, a part of the bureaucracy that in theory regulates an industry actually functions as a government representative of the interests of that industry.

Bureaucratic organizations do not offer their services for sale in a competitive marketplace; the bureaucracy serves all eligible citizens without additional charge, because the citizens have already paid for its benefits through their taxes. In a free marketplace, an individual can express his needs and preferences by purchasing one kind of service rather than another, or by refusing to purchase some service if its price seems too high. Because the bureaucracy operates outside the free marketplace, it is impossible to discover whether the bureaucracy is meeting the needs and desires of citizens at a cost they are willing to pay. Citizens can express their approval or disapproval of the government services only very indirectly, by voting for or against particular candidates for public office. The meaning of these votes is greatly diluted because each candidate is also being judged for his positions on a variety of other matters of public policy.

When a company supplies goods or services to customers, it receives immediate feedback through its success in selling; it learns what kinds of goods and services the customers want and what prices they are willing to pay. The business is forced to be reasonably efficient in its operation; if it is not, a competitor will be able to offer the same goods or services at lower cost and therefore will win away its customers. These arguments do not apply to the bureaucratic government agency that operates outside the free marketplace. Hence, bureaucracies are unlikely to make efficient use of available resources or to allocate their resources in the way that the citizenry might wish. A bureaucratic agency tends to flourish if it pleases certain political leaders who control its budget, so its policies are tailored to please those leaders rather than to meet the needs of the citizens that it serves. Thus citizens may get more national defense and less public health care than they need or want. The problem is further complicated by the predominant view that the extent of needs for services such as national defense can be accurately judged only by those experts who hold positions in the bureaucracy.

Judging whether an agency's budget is too large or too small is a difficult (if not impossible) task, and yet these budgets tend to grow larger over the years. There are several reasons for the seemingly inevitable, often unnecessary expansion of bureaucracies. Any agency is created as a response to a public demand for certain programs; the supporters of these programs desire large quantities of the service offered by the agency. Congressmen elected by these political sectors favor increased budgets for the agency in order to maintain their popularity among their consituents. Exchanges take place between voters and legislators, between legislators and bureaucrats, and between bureaucrats and citizens. Those citizens and legislators who have no interest in the agency's programs often play no role in the bargaining about the agency's budget. Therefore, the outcome of the series of exchanges may be a taxing of disinterested citizens to provide services that the citizens do not need.

Members of a bureaucracy have a natural desire to increase the size, budget, and responsibility of their own agency, because this expansion is likely to increase the status and salary of their own positions. Government bureaucrats actively seek support both in Congress and among the general public in order to increase their share of the budget and the number of their programs. They obtain additional political resources from the support of industries that will benefit by the expanded bureaucratic expenditures. These industries often are able to manipulate considerable political power in dealing with particular legislators, either through campaign support or because employees and customers of the industry cast a significant proportion of the votes in the legislator's district. Alliances among bureaucrats, businessmen, and legislators often are formed to the mutual benefit of these leaders, but such alliances often result in policies that do not enhance the general welfare of the citizenry. For example, the public transportation system in the United States has been allowed to deteriorate since World War II in large part because the automobile and trucking industries have wielded sufficient economic and political power to draw the attention and resources of the government away from public transportation. The Highway Trust Fund was established under the Eisenhower administration to advance the cause of highway construction. The fund is financed by taxation of gasoline, so the cost burden is borne directly by the users of highways. However, an indirect cost burden is placed upon the entire society through neglect of mass transportation, demolition of neighborhoods and communities for highways construction, damage done to places of natural beauty, pollution, and congestion.

As the highway system expanded, sales of automobiles increased; increasing use of automobiles led to demand and funds for further highway construction. New places of business and public facilities were designed for convenient access by automobile, while public transportation was often unable to obtain funds to expand to serve new developments. In many areas, most citizens found it necessary to own an automobile in order to carry out their daily activities. Once they owned an automobile, they found it more economical and convenient to use the car for all transportation. As use of public transit facilities declined, budgets for those services declined and it became more and more difficult to provide adequate service. Thus, a vicious circle was created that tended to increase automobile traffic and force the deterioration of public transportation systems.

The automobile, oil, tire, and construction industries profited from the expansion of the highway system, as did the administrators of the program and the congressmen who traded support with the administrators and industries. However, the great increase in automobile traffic led to extreme multiplication of all the negative side effects upon the general society. As these costs have become more extreme and obvious, the public has begun to demand a cutback in highway expenditures and an increase in government support for public transportation systems. This example illustrates the difficulty of judging the success and efficiency of a bureaucratic program. In the case of the highway program, the social and economic consequences were not perceived or understood until many years after the program was put into operation.

POLITICAL PARTIES

The expansion of the right to vote in America and later in Great Britain led to the creation of modern political parties—organized groups that have as their primary purpose the mobilization of large numbers of votes to support particular candidates who will attain public office and influence public policy. In the early stages of American and British democracy, only males of relatively high socioeconomic status were able to vote; the voting population was relatively small and homogeneous. As nonlandowners, women, blacks, and other groups gained the right to vote, political parties came into existence to provide political bargaining power for various viewpoints within the society. The nature of the complex party system that has formed in each modern democracy has its roots in the specific historical evolution of each nation. In general, parties have formed as a result of conflicts between the culturally dominant and the culturally subordinant—or between any coalitions of these factions. As particular conflicts have lost intensity or relevance, political parties and systems have evolved to represent contemporary conflicts within each society. Sometimes old parties are replaced by new ones; sometimes parties shift their positions drastically within the system; sometimes the entire system of parties changes to a form that is unrecognizably different from the old one. The study of the origins and evolution of parties is beyond our scope here; we will use the exchange model to discuss the dynamics of political parties, with particular emphasis on the American party system.

The American political experience is an unusual one in that a fairly equal competition exists between the two largest parties for the votes of individual citizens. In most other countries, the system either is dominated by a single party or includes more than two significant parties. Among countries with two-party systems, the United States is unusual in that its two present parties have been in continuous existence as the major parties for a very long time.

Each of the two American political parties—Democratic and Republican—is a coalition of diverse political sectors. In part these coalitions are the result of policies currently adopted by the parties, and in part they are remnants of past events and policies. The larger of the two parties, the Democratic party, is a loose coalition that tends to attract Southerners, various ethnic minority groups, Catholics (particularly those of Irish and Eastern European descent), Jews, blacks, union members, farmers, urban residents, and intellectuals. The

Republican party is a similarly loose coalition that tends to attract upper-income WASPs (white, Anglo-Saxon Protestants), business executives, Catholics of German descent, Lutherans, Presbyterians, and residents of suburbs and small towns. Neither party has a majority of registered voters; thus each party seeks to attract particular sectors into its coalition by promising its efforts to obtain policies and programs desired by those sectors. In other words, each party seeks enough votes to put its candidates into office by espousing certain policies designed to build a winning coalition.

The Democratic party tends to promise a major role for the national government in the economy (strong anti-trust action, active regulation of big business, and governmental provision of those goods and services neglected by private enterprise), programs for the poor and for minority groups, and programs favored by labor. The Republican party tends to promise a reduced role for the national government in the economic marketplace, reduced social programs on the national level, increased autonomy for state and local governments, and programs favored by big business. However, observers of the American political scene soon note that there is very little dramatic change in public policy when one party takes power from the other. In practice, each party must retain some support from the sectors represented by the other party and must obtain strong support from sectors not closely associated with either party if it is to remain in power. Therefore, both parties in fact tend to establish similar public policies aimed at giving something to each political sector and avoiding serious alienation of any important sector.

For example, although the Republican party is often described as the party of business, many business leaders belong to the Democratic party. Either party will take many actions favorable to business when it is in power. Certain companies or industries may fare better under one party or the other because of political bargains they have made with a particular party, but business as a whole tends to do quite well for itself with the leadership of either party. The support of the business community is crucial to the functioning of any government, so any party in power must offer sufficient benefits to obtain that support.

Because the two major American parties do represent complex coalitions drawn from all sectors of the society and because both parties seek to hold the support of a majority of the voters, it often seems that there is little real difference between the policies enacted by political leaders from the two parties. It would be difficult in many cases to determine the party to which a politician belongs by an analysis of his positions on various issues. So-called "conservative" Democrats often seem more closely allied with "conservative" Republicans than with "liberal" Democrats. As a result, voters often complain that they have no real choice between the parties and that they have no way to cast a vote that would make clear their positions on particular issues.

Each party seeks to create a large body of voters who identify with the party and who will faithfully cast their votes for candidates of the party. In trying to build this strong party identification, parties often appeal to the emotions of the voter rather than to any rational calculation he might make about costs and benefits. The voter who commits himself to party loyalty exchanges his freedom of choice for the benefit of psychological comfort; he puts his trust in the leaders of the party and is relieved of the burden of fully examining each issue and candidate in terms of his own benefits and costs. In many cases, a voter learns as a child to identify himself with the party of his parents and retains this identification for life.

For the party, voter loyalty reduces both costs and uncertainty. Costs decrease because the party need not spend large sums of money in disseminating information to educate voters on issues and candidates. Uncertainty is reduced because the party knows that it can always count on a certain minimal percentage of the citizenry— the party regulars. It can then focus its resources and attention on attracting enough additional votes from uncommitted voters and from voters associated with the other party to put together a winning total.

In the two-party system, the political market is imperfect because the individual can choose only between the alternatives offered by the two major parties in terms of candidates and a package of programs. He knows that no minority-party candidate is likely to win in any contest for an important office, so he feels that his vote will be meaningful only in helping to influence the choice between the two major parties. Neither party is likely to promise a public policy that is very close to the policy the individual would like to obtain. However, the two-party system does offer a benefit to the individual by reducing his decision-making costs. He need not spend time, money, or energy in the pursuit of political information that will be of little practical use to him. He can merely determine which party offers a program closer to the one he desires, and then he can support the candidates of that party with little further effort.

Legal and institutional factors reinforce this imperfect market for political parties and increase the costs of entrance for other potential parties. At the presidential level, the electoral-college system tends to perpetuate the two-party system. In most cases, all of the electoral votes of a state go to the candidate receiving the largest number of popular votes in that state. This winner-take-all system makes it impossible for any candidate to attain the presidency unless he represents a coalition of many political sectors. For example, a party strongly representing one large political sector might win a sizeable minority of votes in every state, but fail to obtain a single electoral vote for its candidate because that political sector would not represent a majority of the popular vote in any one state. Thus, Robert LaFollette (presidential candidate of the Progressive party in 1924) received 17 percent of the popular vote across the nation, but was able to obtain only 2.5 percent of the vote in the electoral college. The major parties tend to focus their efforts on obtaining winning popular votes in the most populous states, which control the largest number of votes in the electoral college. In 1972, a party could have obtained a majority in the electoral college by wining the popular vote in only the 11 largest of the 50 states. The political sectors strongly represented in the voting populations of these large states therefore hold very strong bargaining positions in the political marketplace.

The effectiveness of the electoral-college system in eliminating minority parties may be judged by the fact that every presidential election in more than a century has been won by either the Republican or the Democratic candidate. Today there is a growing tendency for voters to identify themselves as independents or to identify with minority parties. If the major parties do not succeed in wooing most of the voters back into their coalitions, it is possible that some third party will eventually put together a coalition that can win the presidency. However, history shows that such an event inevitably leads to the rapid decline and disappearance of one of the former major parties, and thus to the restoration of the two-party system with its large political coalitions.

Congressional elections do not involve a winner-take-all mechanism like the electoral college. Each candidate must obtain a plurality of the vote in a district (for Congress) or a state (for the Senate) in order to attain office. In theory, many parties could compete in these elections. In practice, however, coalitions tend to form around the organizations provided by the national parties. Suppose that five parties did compete for a congressional seat in some district; the winner might receive only slightly more than 20 percent of the vote. Almost certainly, two or more of the parties would form a coalition in the next election in an effort to ensure victory. This process would be likely to continue until only two large coalition parties are left. In practice, because the major-party coalitions are already established, minority parties have little reason to invest resources against their slim chances of winning office. Where more than two parties do exist locally (in New York, for example), preelection exchanges of endorsements usually take place so that only two major candidates backed by various party coalitions appear on the ballot.

State laws regulate access to the ballot, and these laws have been written by the members of the parties in power. Naturally, these laws tend to discourage the appearance of other parties on the ballot, by increasing the political costs associated with qualifying for the ballot any candidate not affiliated with one of the two major parties. Furthermore, two of the major ingredients for electoral success in the United States are adequate financial resources and access to the media. Most groups and individuals with large amounts of money to invest in political campaigns are already associated with one or both of the major-party coalitions; the major parties promise them significant benefits in return for their financial support. They are very unlikely to shift their support to a third party because there is little chance that such a party could win. They have no reason to risk losing a favored position in a major-party coalition for the very slim possibility of winning a better position with a third party. Similarly, the media tend to give little attention to candidates not affiliated with the two major parties; because such candidates have little chance of winning, their statements and activities are not very important as news. Federal laws requiring that media give equal time to all candidates have actually tended to favor the two-party system. The media do not want to devote much time or space to minor candidates because they feel that they are of little interest to the public; therefore, they reduce their electoral coverage in general. Paid political advertising has become the major source of political information for the citizen—and of course the major parties have the financial resources to dominate such advertising overwhelmingly.

New laws providing public funds to finance campaigns also tend to favor major parties (because other parties find it very difficult to qualify for the funds), as do recent reforms limiting campaign expenditures (because incumbents are already well-known to voters, while minor-party candidates would need to spend large sums on advertising to make themselves and their positions known). Thus we see that a number of legal and institutional factors built into the structure of the political marketplace impose heavy costs on potential entrants to the marketplace who seek to compete with the two major parties. These factors reduce competition in the marketplace and limit the choices available to the individual voter.

We must return to the issue of conflict to appreciate fully the role of the political party in modern society. Political parties provide the mechanism that rechannels conflicts about the allocation of scarce resources, translating public demands into government actions without the violence of riot or rebellion. If a voter identifies himself with one of the major parties, he is likely to feel that his viewpoint is being heard by the government. The two parties fairly regularly exchange places in control of the government, so the voter always knows that his party will soon have a chance to exercise power if it is not doing so at the moment.

The appearance of violence or other antisystemic activity can be taken as an indication that the party system has failed to translate political demands into realistic programs. This might occur if a party fails to deliver on the promises it has made to some sector within its coalition, or if some sector comes to feel that neither major party is making significant promises to it. The disgruntled sector may feel excluded from any chance of influencing public policy through the party system and that antisystemic action offers a better chance of success, even though the costs are high. In many cases, a disgruntled sector turns to a third party to express its demands. Even though the chance of electoral success is slim, the public attention and demonstration of electoral strength by the third party is likely to cause the major parties to offer better bargains to draw the alienated sector back into one coalition or the other.

Over the past century, the coalitions represented by the Republican and Democratic parties have shifted as changes occurred in the social and economic system. For example, railroads and steel companies once tended to play major roles within the party coalitions. Today, defense industries and automobile and oil companies are more important powers in the coalitions. Only if one of the major-party coalitions fails to change its policies and promises enough to keep the support of a significant group of political sectors will a new party have a chance of replacing it. Because many voters now feel that their interests are not being represented by either party, many attempts to build third parties are being made. In each case, a few dissatisfied political sectors are chosen as a central base with hopes of attracting enough other sectors away from the major parties to create a viable new major party. If the history of the past century is any guide, however, the most likely outcome will be a shifting of power within the major parties to grant increased satisfaction to the sectors that are becoming more important (with a corresponding decline in the benefits promised to once-important sectors that are now fading in political or economic power); the unhappy sectors will be offered better bargains that will draw them back into the existing major parties. Serious disruption of the political system (revolutionary change) could occur only if significant political sectors were completely excluded from any reasonable chance of obtaining benefits through the party system, and the nature of the system makes it very unlikely that such sectors will be excluded for long. Because the two major parties are roughly equal in political strength, each seeks to attract support from any dissatisfied group in order to give itself the slight additional support needed to attain power.

INTEREST GROUPS

Interest groups (or political sectors) are groups of citizens sharing common viewpoints and objectives. An interest group becomes significant only when it forms some sort of organization that can act as its bargaining agent in the political marketplace. Among the many interest groups in our complex society are organizations of farmers, workers, industries, professions, consumers, environmentalists, and so on. An individual joins such an organization because he expects it to provide benefits greater than the costs he incurs by joining. The major political benefit is the fact that the organization can use the pooled resources of its members to exert enhanced political leverage. An individual farmer could not exert much bargaining power in the political marketplace, but a large group of farmers can offer enough votes and campaign resources to attract promises of desired benefits from many candidates. The interest group differs from a political party because it represents only one particular part of the society and therefore is not in a position to present candidates who can attract enough votes to win elections. Instead, the interest group argues strongly for its own viewpoint and seeks to exert its influence as part of the coalition that makes up a party. The greater the political resources that the interest group can offer to the party, the more closely the party program is likely to match the desires of the interest group. Always implicit in this intraparty bargaining is the threat that the interest group will shift its political resources to the other major party if its demands are not sufficiently satisfied. If the interest group has enough political resources, it can strike bargains with both parties. The threat of shifting all support to the other party is enough to obtain significant benefits from both parties; thus the powerful interest group is assured of benefits no matter which party happens to be in power at a given time.

Within the United States, one of the most successful interest groups has been the American Medical Association. For several decades, this organization of medical professionals has had the legal right to approve programs of medical schools and to judge the qualifications of prospective doctors. Thus the medical profession has regulated legal access to its ranks and has controlled the supply of doctors. In addition, the AMA has the power to administer severe sanctions against deviant members through the state medical boards. Naturally, limitations upon the supply of doctors and upon competition between doctors has increased doctors' incomes and has had important effects upon the cost of health care to the American citizen. The maintenance of high incomes for doctors is the major service that the AMA renders its members in exchange for their dues and loyalty.

Like the AMA, other interest groups try to shape public policy to insure maximum benefits for their members, seeking to structure the distribution of advantages and disadvantages in a favorable manner. Local craft unions were formed very early in the history of the United States, but labor groups did not become really significant on the national political scene until the Knights of Labor appeared as a public organization in 1880. After many decades of struggle, the labor movement finally succeeded in 1935 in obtaining passage of the Wagner–Connery Act, designed to eliminate legal restraints on unionization, greatly reducing the heavy costs previously associated with union activity. The labor movement was successful because it was able to deliver large blocks of votes (and large amounts of campaign support) to those political leaders who would reciprocate by supporting legislation that altered the distribution of rewards in a direction more favorable to the union movement.

In our own time, black leaders have organized their community to press for changes in the American political system. The Voting Rights Act of 1965 is a classic case of legislation intended to alter the balance of bargaining in the political marketplace—in this case, the bargaining relationship of whites and blacks in the southern states. This act significantly altered the distribution of political advantage that had for so long given whites a great advantage in the South. The civil rights movement was able to achieve this objective because of the large numbers of both white and black citizens that it mobilized in support of political candidates commited to this policy goal.

The building trade unions provide another example of successful action by an interest group in recent times. Like the AMA, these unions have sought to limit access to the market in which they compete and to maintain the existing balance of supply in the marketplace. The unions control entrance into their labor market through the closed shop and the apprentice system. No union will allow its members to work on a construction project unless all workers on the job are union members; an individual can become a union member only by serving as an apprentice in the educational system set up by the union. The relatives of union members have been given preference in admission to the apprentice system, so that blacks and other members of minority groups have rarely been able to become union members (at least until very recently). The building trade unions have also succeeded in using their political resources to obtain building codes that require contractors to make maximal use of union members' services on any construction job. The unions have strongly opposed attempts to alter these codes to permit use of new techniques and materials that might eliminate jobs for union members or reduce the number of man-hours required to construct a building. Among the externalities generated by the unions' successful use of their political power are high costs for the consumer and a continuing housing shortage.

In the United States, the terms "lobby" and "lobbying" are used to describe the efforts of political sectors to influence legislators. Lobbying is an activity recognized as a normal part of the political system; it is one of the means by which political leaders learn about the demands of various sectors. Interest groups formally organize lobbying activities to channel support or threats of sanctions to public officials, and also to process demands from their members. This flow of information between citizens and government through lobbying cuts the cost of government. Without this service, decision-making costs would increase as the chances of mistaken decisions based on imperfect information would sharply increase. Lobbying also serves political leaders by decreasing uncertainty about the kinds of policy proposals that will receive approval from significant parts of the citizenry. With this knowledge, leaders take less risk of losing political support by investing their resources in commitments that will fail or will jeopardize their popularity. Finally, information provided by lobbying serves as a check on bureaucracy by signaling the political leadership when the bureaucracy fails to supply efficiently and honestly the services that the leadership intended and that the citizen expects.

Political sectors generally are significant only when they are represented by a strong organization. Politicians may try to offer benefits to less organized groups (such as "the Italian-American vote" or "the youth vote"), but in the absence of organized lobbying it is very difficult for the leader to know what benefits the group actually desires or to obtain much organized political support from the group. Recent attempts to organize political groups of consumers, environmentalists, and "well-informed citizens" are based upon recognition of the need for organization if any group is to deal effectively in our political marketplace. One disadvantage of the lobbying system is that a powerful organization may not always accurately communicate the demands of its members. An individual doctor or member of a building trades union may disagree with the demands voiced by the organization that speaks for him, but he must continue to support that organization if he is to keep his job.

Like so many other aspects of politics, interest groups can augment the legitimacy of the political system if individuals are satisfied with the benefits received in relation to the costs of belonging to the organization, if the probability of shaping public policy in desired directions is perceived to be high, and if the benefits that the organization obtains are rewarding to its members. In this case, the individual member will find satisfaction in his participation in the political process through membership in the organization. However, because interest groups play such major roles in political bargaining, those individuals who have no organization to speak for their interests may feel unable to influence the government through their votes and political support of candidates; such individuals are likely to view the system as illegitimate if they are unable to find or organize an interest group to speak for them.

PUBLIC OPINION

The term "public opinion" refers to the viewpoints held by a significant portion of the citizenry, as determined through elections, polls, statements and activities of interest groups, and less formal samplings of individual opinions. Citizens express their opinions on various issues, expecting their political leaders to take these opinions into account when acting on public issues and policies. In practice, we can define public opinion as that set of viewpoints that political leaders consider important when deciding how to act on political questions.

In his broadest sense, public opinion is the information available to the political leadership about the needs and demands of the citizenry. This information can be regarded as a political resource. It is useful to distinguish two categories of public opinion: prescriptive and permissive. Prescriptive public opinion represents a demand for some particular action—for example, a demand that welfare costs be reduced or a demand that better programs of pollution control be enacted. In a sense, such prescriptive opinion is a negative resource for the leader; it limits his freedom to act as he might wish and requires him to make decisions that will satisfy the demands of the citizens. On the other hand, permissive public opinion represents a feeling that certain actions would be acceptable, though they are not demanded—for example, the viewpoint that legalized abortion would be acceptable, or that there would be no major objection to the imposition of certain tariffs on imported goods. Permissive public opinion is a positive resource for the political leader; it enables him to offer certain benefits to win the support of particular political sectors, knowing that he will not lose support from other parts of the citizenry by doing so.

The question of American policy toward the People's Republic of China (Communist China) provides a good recent example of the dual nature of public opinion. Throughout this century, American public opinion has generally been strongly opposed to Communist movements and governments. In part, this public opinion developed because citizens granted legitimacy to the government of the United States, and therefore opposed a movement that announced the overthrow of that government as its goal. However, this public opinion also was partly created and amplified through the efforts of political leaders who found it useful. In general, the leaders wanted a permissive public opinion that would support any decision by the government if that decision were explained as an act against Communism. Particularly during the 1950s, leaders were able to make many policy decisions aimed at improving their own political strength (for example, by giving various benefits to defense industries) and then to defuse any opposition to these decisions by giving an anti-Communist justification. However, the public opinion also had a prescriptive dimension; the citizenry demanded that steps be taken to oppose Communism and refused to support actions viewed as favorable to Communist interests.

During the 1960s, it became clear to many political leaders that there was no longer any realistic hope of restoring mainland China to non-Communist government. Furthermore, the leaders realized that better relationships with Communist China would be useful in creating a world balance of power more favorable to American interests. However, over the preceding decade the leadership had convinced the general public (and many leaders as well) of the evil results that would follow from any normal intercourse with the Communist Chinese government. The prescriptive demand for anti-Communist actions proved for many years to be a restraint on the development of realistic policies. American Presidents feared that their opponents would benefit politically if the Presidents took any initiatives toward better relationships with China, or even if they made any attempt to change public opinion through education. In order to win public support, these Presidents even found themselves forced to make statements opposing friendship with China, thus reinforcing the public opinion that restricted their freedom to act.

Ironically, it was Richard Nixon—one of the leaders of the anti-Communist political campaign in the 1950s—who did reverse the long-standing policy and initiate more normal relationships with the Communist government of China. In part, he felt able to do so because his reputation as an opponent of Communism was so well-established that the public would not view his action as a capitulation. His action was also made possible by the changes in public opinion resulting from the war in Vietnam. The failure of American military might to eliminate a Communist government in a small and relatively poor country led to a general public recognition of the impossibility of driving the Communist government out of power in China. Furthermore, the prescriptive public demand for an end to American involvement in an Asian war led to a permissive opinion that would tolerate almost any act aimed at maintaining peace in Asia. This example emphasizes the fact that public opinion is a resource for any leader when he can rally it to the support of his position; but it is a restraint on his freedom of action when he cannot. It can be argued that both Lyndon Johnson and Richard Nixon were forced to give up the presidency when they failed to find suitable policies that would satisfy the demands of public opinion.

Information is power, and those who control information have an important resource at their disposal. Political systems may be classified according to the role of public opinion and the extent to which any political sector (including the government) monopolizes the control of information flow within the system. Even the most autocratic regime pays lip service to public opinion, but information in such a political system is monopolized by one or a few political sectors and is controlled in order to mold public opinion to desired patterns. Competitive opinions or sources of information are suppressed.

The hallmark of a democratic regime is the existence of a free market for information. In such a system, public opinion is not molded by the government but emerges from the competition of ideas in the free marketplace. Laws and rules are designed to keep the system open to all sources of information and to eliminate any structural features that would impede the free flow of information. There are few, if any, sanctions against the dissemination of information, and no heavy costs are placed on those who attempt to influence public opinion. The Constitution of the United States clearly represents an attempt to construct a political system close to this democratic ideal.

However, in any actual political system, various political sectors (including the government) do exert some control over the market for information. Since World War II, political leaders in the United States have often used the threat of subversion and espionage as a justification for the suppression of information. In the 1960s and 1970s, for example, the United States conducted and financed an extensive war against Communist forces in Laos. Presidents and other leaders not only suppressed information about this war but also made false statements denying its existence. This action was justified (among the leaders at the time, and in statements to the public after information leaked out) on the grounds that public knowledge of the war would have provided aid to the enemy. However, since the enemy obviously knew much more about the war than did the American public, it seems clear that the leaders controlled the information flow in order to protect themselves from adverse public reactions that they expected if the details of the war were known to the voters in the United States. The Watergate scandal of the early 1970s provides many examples of ways in which political leaders manipulated information in order to conceal illegal, incompetent or corrupt activities within the government. Clearly, the United States political system does not provide the completely free exchange of information that is called for by the democratic ideal.

VOTING

Voting in elections is an activity usually regarded as characteristic of a democratic system, but some form of voting exists in most non-democratic systems as well. Our discussion here is in some respects a continuation of our early treatment of political parties, but here we focus on the behavior of individuals rather than on the structure of organizations. We first undertake a general analysis of individual political behavior, and then look more closely at American voting behavior.

If we ignore for the moment the irrational elements that influence all human behavior, we may view the average voter simply as a person who seeks to maximize his benefits and minimize his costs. The political party or candidate makes policy commitments, offering certain benefits in exchange for support from the citizen. The individual chooses from among the various programs offered to him and casts his vote for the candidate or party that seems to offer the better bargain. If the bargain seems good enough, he may invest even more than his vote by offering money, time, or other resources to help the candidate or party obtain other votes.

Of course, the voter must also take into account the probability that his preferred candidate or party will win the election. For example, suppose that candidates A, B, and C are running for the same office in a given election. A voter concludes that candidate C offers the program that will be most beneficial to his own interests, that candidate B offers an acceptable program, and that candidate A promises a program that would be totally unacceptable. It would seem at first glance that the individual should vote for C. However, suppose that other information available convinces him that C has no chance of winning the election; it will be a close race between A and B. In this case, he may well conclude that the best investment of his vote and other resources is in support of candidate B. He cannot hope to obtain the benefits promised by C, but he can at least hope to avoid the negative results expected if A wins.

Such a complex analysis is quite logical, but the typical voter seldom carries through such an analysis in detail. To make such an analysis in a real situation would require a great deal of information; the gathering and processing of such information usually requires an investment of time and money. The voter must balance the benefits to be obtained from the analysis (leading to the best possible use of his vote) against the cost of making the analysis. He may conclude that the effort is not worthwhile, or he may make a less thorough analysis involving a smaller cost to himself. Without a thorough analysis, the individual may decide that he has no way to cast a meaningful vote; he is just as likely to do himself harm as to help himself, because he is not sure which candidate he should support. Even if he expects a fair chance of some benefit from the vote, he may decide that the cost (in time, energy, or even salary) of voting outweighs the expected benefit. Only when he perceives his vote as highly significant in terms of his own welfare is the individual likely to incur the costs of voting. Of course, as mentioned in an earlier chapter, the act of voting may carry other benefits (such as status within the community or a sense of psychological satisfaction in following habit or tradition) that justify its costs, even when the voter feels that his vote itself is relatively meaningless.

Turning from this theoretical analysis to actual American elections, we note that many citizens apparently conclude that the expected benefits of voting do not justify its costs. Table 1 shows that from 37 to 49 percent of the voting-age population has failed to cast votes in presidential elections over the past few decades. Of course, some of these individuals were ineligible to vote because of recent changes in residence, lack of citizenship, and so on. Others may have been prevented from voting by illness, bad weather, or emergencies. However, most of them chose not to incur the cost of voting. Note that the percentage of adults failing to vote is larger than the percentage voting for the winner in every election. Results of congressional elections show even less voter participation.

Why do so many Americans choose not to participate in elections? A more detailed analysis would show that voter participa-

Table 1
Participation in recent American presidential elections

	Percentage of Voting-Age Population		
Year	Not Voting	Voting for Democrat	Voting for Republican
1932	47.6	30.0	20.8
1936	43.1	34.6	20.8
1940	41.1	32.2	26.4
1944	44.0	29.9	25.8
1948	48.9	25.4	23.0
1952	38.4	27.4	34.0
1956	40.7	24.9	34.0
1960	37.2	31.2	31.1
1964	38.2	37.8	23.8
1968	39.1	26.0	26.4
1972	44.3	20.8	33.8

Source: Adapted from **The Statistical Abstract of the U.S.**, 94th ed., Bureau of the Census, U.S. Department of Commerce, 1973.

tion is smallest among the lower socioeconomic groups in the society (Figure 3). Millions of poor Americans and members of low-status minority groups apparently perceive the costs of voting as larger than the expected benefits. They may conclude that neither party offers a program that would significantly alter the distribution of resources in their favor. Members of the higher socioeconomic strata participate to a much larger extent in voting, indicating that these individuals do receive and appreciate benefits from voting—benefits that significantly outweigh the costs of voting.

Analyses of election results often emphasize apparently nonrational explanations for voter behavior. Voters are said to be swayed by slick advertising campaigns, by glamor and charisma of candidates, or by irrational fears of crime in the streets or black power. In most cases, the behavior of the individual voter is more rational than it might appear at first glance. An outside observer might conclude that the individual has not cast his vote in the most rational manner—that he has not voted for the candidate who offers him the greatest benefits. However, the individual's decision usually appears quite rational if viewed in the framework of the information available to him and the potential benefits that he values.

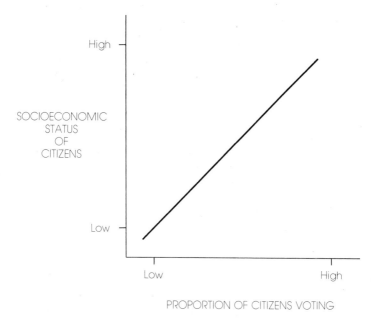

High —

SOCIOECONOMIC
STATUS
OF
CITIZENS

Low —

Low   High

PROPORTION OF CITIZENS VOTING

Figure 3
Participation in elections in the United States varies with socioeconomic
status. The fact that millions of poor citizens do not vote has been
attributed to their perception that neither major party represents their
interests.

The voter who casts a straight party ticket may vote for some
candidates who do not seem the best for his interests. However, he
may be acting quite rationally in cutting his information-gathering costs
by trusting the party's selection, feeling that the risk of misusing his
vote is not large enough to justify the cost of fully investigating all
candidates. Furthermore, he may receive other benefits (such as
status or even a good government job) as rewards for his party loyalty.
The voter who is influenced by an advertising campaign may similarly be making the rational choice to minimize his costs by using the
information readily available. The voters who participate in so-called
"backlashes" against crime or black power are probably acting
rationally upon the information that they have obtained for the investment they chose to make in obtaining information. Many
analyses have suggested that those voting for George Wallace in 1968
were acting irrationally, voting for a man whose policies would

damage them simply because they approved of his opposition to long-hairs, blacks, and welfare chislers. However, the votes for Wallace could equally well be explained by saying that these individuals perceived very high future costs for themselves if black Americans were given more advantages and if government social programs continued to expand. Seeing these costs as far greater than the perceived costs to them of other parts of Wallace's program, they made a rational decision in choosing to vote for Wallace.

It is sometimes argued that voters act irrationally when they waste their vote on a third-party candidate who has no realistic chance of winning. However, the significant vote cast for Wallace in 1968 created a significant stock of political capital which Wallace used to influence the Nixon administration. In planning its strategy for the 1972 election campaign, the Nixon organization concluded that it needed the votes of the Southerners and blue-collar workers who had voted for Wallace in 1968. In order to attract those voters to the support of Nixon, the administration made many policy decisions that were in accord with the program advocated by Wallace. The Democratic party also made certain concessions to the Wallace supporters in an attempt to compete for their support. Again we must conclude that individual voter behavior can be explained as the result of a logical choice; the demonstration of popular support for Wallace's program did lead to desired shifts in public policy, even though Wallace was unable to win the election.

Legal and institutional aspects of the political system sometimes play an important role in an individual's decision whether to vote. In the United States, each state structures election laws within certain limits prescribed by the national government and the Constitution. Various state laws setting requirements for residency, literacy, voting registration, hours of polling, the form of the ballot, and qualification of candidates for listing on the ballot have all been used at one time or another to control or limit access to the election process. Restrictions on the right to vote have usually served to increase the costs of voting for the least privileged members of society. Restrictions on candidates' access to a ballot listing have limited the choices for all voters, but in most cases these restrictions are designed to have little effect on the candidates favored by the more privileged sectors. We have already noted one important result of these restrictions: the less privileged members of the society are quite likely to make the rational decision that the costs of voting outweigh the expected benefits, and therefore to stay away from the polls.

Other important aspects of the American political structure are the two-party system (with its emphasis upon coalitions of interest groups and upon lobbying) and the uneven distribution of political resources in the society. An individual of high socioeconomic status has enough resources to make the cost of political participation seem quite small. His chances of obtaining significant benefits are enhanced by the fact that he can invest more resources, thus winning a better bargain from the candidate he supports. Furthermore, he has good reason to help support the system and keep it functioning in its present form, because he is already receiving above-average benefits from the system.

Americans of lower socioeconomic status are likely to perceive the political process as irrelevant to their lives. They have few political resources to invest and therefore are unable to win significant promises of benefits if they offer their support to a particular candidate. Because their resources are small, the cost of voting or other participation in politics seems very high. These individuals are likely to seek benefits through organizations and activities that lie outside the political system. Because they receive a below-average share of the society's resources, they are likely to be dissatisfied with the political system; however, they are also likely to view themselves as powerless to bring about any change in the system. They regard the competition between the two major parties as collusive maneuvering among those who already control the political marketplace and who effectively exclude from the marketplace any competing interests that might alter the balance of power. Therefore most lower class Americans conclude that both systemic and antisystemic activities are unlikely to bring them any benefits; they focus their resources upon asystemic activities that can bring them at least some benefits.

REFERENCES

Down, Anthony. *An Economic Theory of Democracy*. New York: Harper & Row, 1957.

Eisenstein, James. *Politics and the Legal Process*. New York: Harper & Row, 1973.

Frohlich, Norman, Joe A. Oppenheimer, and Oran R. Young. *Political Leadership and Collective Goods*. Princeton, N. J.: Princeton Univ. Press, 1971.

Hargrove, Erwin. *The Power of the Modern Presidency.* New York: Random House, 1974.

Hirschman, Albert O. *Exit, Voice and Loyalty.* Cambridge, Mass.: Harvard Univ. Press, 1970.

Illchman, Warren F. and Norman Thomas Uphoff. *The Political Economy of Change.* Berkeley: Univ. of California Press, 1971.

Key, V. O., Jr. *Politics, Parties, and Pressure Groups.* New York: Crowell, 1964.

_____ *Public Opinion and American Democracy.* New York: Knopf, 1961.

Niskanen, William A., Jr. *Bureaucracy and Representative Government.* Chicago: Aldine-Atherton, 1971.

Olsen, Moncur. *The Logic of Collective Actions.* New York: Schocken, 1965.

Parenti, Michael. *Democracy for the Few.* New York: St. Martin's Press, 1974.

Rieselbach Leroy N. *Congressional Politics.* New York: McGraw-Hill, 1973.

Tullock, Gordon. *Private Wants, Public Means.* New York: Basic Books, 1970.

Political Exchange: A Comparative Perspective

Chapter 3 presented many generalizations about political leadership, legislators, bureaucracy, political parties, and elections, particularly as they exist in the political system of the United States. The broad analysis of these topics can be applied to any industrial competitive political system. In this chapter, we use the exchange model to compare and contrast various national political systems. In particular, we draw a distinction between competitive and noncompetitive political systems among the industrialized nations. We also examine political systems of the Third World, attempting to analyze political modernization in terms of the exchange model.

INDUSTRIAL COMPETITIVE SYSTEMS

A competitive political system (or marketplace) is one in which many groups and individuals (that is, political sectors and political entre-preneurs) seek to trade scarce political resources (power, prestige, wealth, status, and so on) for political support. Many different groups enter the marketplace with various stocks of political resources; in the market, they strike bargains with other groups and individuals, seeking to invest their resources in ways that will bring them increased resources, usually by influencing public policy. Individual entrepreneurs enter the marketplace, seeking to mobilize support from the interest groups in order to win governmental office. They promise particular positions on public policy in return for political resources given in their support.

The free competitive market is characterized by a large number of traders (each with a stock of resources and support to trade) and by relatively easy access at relatively low cost. No one group or individual can structure the marketplace to exclude other groups or individuals, and the structure of costs and benefits is roughly the same for any group seeking to participate in the political exchange. In the United States, the basic structure of the political marketplace is set forth in the Constitution, but many important details of the structure are determined by laws, regulations, and traditions. In any legitimate political system, the structure of a fully competitive marketplace must treat all citizens in the same fashion, and all citizens must agree to support the structure. Looking at modern industrialized nations with competitive political systems, we find that the systems differ mostly in details of the market structure and in the particular forms of behavior that are rewarded or discouraged by the system.

As examples, we look here at the political systems of Great Britain, France, and West Germany—particularly at elements of their respective political cultures that contrast with American political culture. (The concept of political culture was discussed in Chapter 1.) In this brief discussion, we focus on the timing and sequence of political revolution and industrialization in these three nations, and on the consequences for their political systems.

In England, national government developed with a structure in which the king shared power with the land-holding nobility. In 1215, a group of rebellious barons forced King John to sign the Magna Carta, which placed restrictions upon the power of the monarch. Later, Parliament was established as a governmental body including both great feudal lords and representatives of other sectors in the society. Because Parliament controlled the power of taxation and could veto legislation imposed by the monarch, a political marketplace was created in which the monarch was forced to bargain with the various sectors represented in Parliament.

At first, Parliament largely represented the interests of the lords, but other sectors gained power in Parliament as they gained economic power in the society. The feudal lords became landlords. tenant farmers worked for wages and paid rent for land; a commercial class of successful farmers came into being. A cloth industry developed, leading to expansion of trade and the economic rise of mill owners, traders, and shippers. Later, exploration and colonial activities accelerated the growth of the commercial and capitalistic sectors. As these changes occurred, the new commercial and capitalistic class (the bourgeoisie) was able to enter the political marketplace and to gain bargaining power in Parliament.

In the seventeenth century, the Stuart kings tried to establish complete control over the political marketplace, but the other political sectors exerted enough bargaining power through Parliament to force changes in public policy. However, many sectors grew increasingly dissatisfied with the influence they were able to obtain through the political structure, and in 1642 the King and Parliament resorted to warfare—the Puritan Revolution and Civil War, which culminated in the beheading of King Charles I, who had been convicted of treason by the Puritan government. The violent conflict continued intermittently until the Glorious Revolution of 1688 finally and firmly established the strong bargaining power of the House of Commons, and the inability of the King to control the political marketplace without concessions to other political sectors.

By the end of the seventeenth century, the English political structure was well-established and possessed a relatively open marketplace. Persons of aristocratic birth, education, or economic power were able to exert bargaining power in the market; they viewed as legitimate the representation of a variety of political interests and the practice of political compromise through bargaining. Late in the eighteenth century, the industrial revolution greatly expanded the size and economic power of the bourgeoisie and brought a large working class into existence. Because the political structure developed through evolution and revolution recognized the desirability of open bargaining in a free political marketplace, these sectors were able to enter the marketplace and exert political power in reasonable proportion to their general standing in the society. Because they were able to exert significant influence on public policy, the new sectors accepted the legitimacy of the political system and rejected the alternative of antisystemic action. The political sectors that had earlier dominated the marketplace ensured their own political survival (albeit with reduced power) by permitting the entry of the new sectors into the marketplace on a relatively equal footing.

In France, national government developed with a succession of very powerful monarchs. While an open political marketplace was developing in England, the trend in France was toward an almost absolute control of the marketplace by the king. Within the formal structure of national government, the king exerted overwhelming control. When commercial and capitalist sectors developed in France as they did in England, these sectors found themselves barred from access to the political marketplace. What power they could exert was exercised through individual bargaining with the monarch, outside the formal marketplace. In such a situation, the powerful monarch was able to exert overwhelming power in each individual bargain, and the other sectors of the society found it very difficult to form coalitions or other wise carry out the kinds of bargaining that would have given them more power in an open market. The rigidity of the political system and a long series of wars brought extreme economic hardship to the French citizenry, along with a growing dissatisfaction with the political system.

The beginnings of industrialization in the late eighteenth century added to the antisystemic feelings, as newly formed political sectors found themselves unable to enter the political marketplace. The Paris parliament rebelled against the absolute power of the monarchy, and the peasantry joined the rebellion in order to shake off the remnants of feudalism that persisted in the inflexible structure. The coincidence of an inflexibly absolutist monarchy, an aristocracy unable to adapt to changing conditions, a large peasantry with small land holdings, and a bourgeoisie seeking political access produced a revolution that swept away the old political system but left a divided tradition in its wake. As the revolution progressed, so did the centralization of government power; increasing demands for equality led to the elimination of most interest groups and the structuring of a political marketplace in which individuals bargained with each other and with the government.

France moved, however haltingly, toward the establishment of a more competitive political system, but the legitimacy of the government has always been questioned by one sector of the society or another. Without a long tradition of political bargaining and compromise, sectors of the French society have often refused to recognize the legitimacy of a government that did not fully meet their demands. Social and economic change has occurred in France, of course, and the public policy has altered as a result of change. However, changes in policy have been strongly opposed by those who perceived change as a cost in the political market, while newly emerging sectors have resorted to antisystemic action when they felt that change was not coming fast enough. The result has been a political culture marked by instability, alienation of the citizenry from the political system, and lagging adaptation of public policy to changing conditions. It has been called a "stalemate" political culture.

Unlike England and France, Germany lacks a long tradition of continuous existence as a national state. The country was long divided into a large number of small monarchies, whose boundaries constantly shifted as a result of wars, alliances, confederations, and the building of empires. In most cases, the monarchs or aristocrats maintained absolute control over the political marketplaces. As in France, the absolutist political systems led to very slow adaptation to changing social and economic conditions. New political sectors found it impossible to enter the political marketplaces. Because of the constant warring among small states, dissatisfied sectors usually offered support to some competing monarch rather than seeking to build a new political system. The only general political tradition that developed was one of obedience to the government while it maintained is absolute power, with a shift of allegiance to any new government that managed to conquer the old.

The revolution of 1848 represented an attempt by the liberal bourgeoisie to unify the nation of Germany under a democratic political system similar to that of France, but the revolution failed. The process of industrialization was already well underway when Bismarck succeeded in unifying Germany under the absolutist monarchical system of Prussia. Under this political system, industrialization proceeded in a manner designed not to undermine the political power of the Prussian aristocracy or to challenge the tradition of obedience to the state. In exchange for their obedience, the bourgeoisie was given economic but not political power. The working class, denied access to the political marketplace, was alienated from the system. The aristocracy maintained its monopoly of such resources as power and status. When a structure of democratic government was finally established in 1919, the antidemocratic and antiliberal political culture persisted to reappear after 1933 in the nightmare of Nazism.

These brief historical sketches illuminate certain elements that differ among the political cultures of three competitive political systems in modern industrialized nations. With this background, we can now turn to some broad comparisons of the systems with each other and with that of the United States. The concept of political culture is useful because it allows us to link the historical evolution of societies to the political behavior of individuals. The political culture conditions a citizen's orientation to his political system, to public policy, and to his own political behavior.

In these three European countries, election participation rarely falls below three-fourths of the enfranchised population. This extensive voter participation in the political marketplace stands in sharp contrast to the behavior of voters in the United States, where we have noted that less than two-thirds of all eligible voters bother to vote in any election. Closer study of voter participation shows that participation varies with social status most markedly in the least class-conscious society of all—the United States. Several explanations have been advanced to account for this seeming discrepancy.

The development of competitive politics in Europe was characterized by the isolation and alienation of the lower classes. In response, these classes developed their own political parties to gain access to the system and to obtain information on the relevance or rewards of political action. These parties formulated policy proposals that appealed to citizens of lower status and, particularly in France and Germany, sought to alter radically the reward structure of the society. Individuals and groups who would lose power as a result of such changes naturally gave their support to political parties that promised to maintain the existing political structure. As a result, the different parties came to offer strongly differing programs for public policy, and individuals tended to identify strongly with the political party that represented their demands. Because a change in the ruling party could bring extreme changes in public policy, voters tend to perceive the outcome of an election as very important to their own interests. The costs of voting are seen as small in comparison to the benefits to be gained if the individual's party obtains power. In the United States, on the other hand, each political sector has some bargaining power with both major parties. Therefore, the voter sees little difference in his own costs or benefits if one party or the other wins.

In France, the divided political culture placed the political parties of the lower classes in the tradition of the revolution and of opposition to the system. This tradition has perpetuated the stalemate in the political marketplace and the perceived legitimacy of direct action and violence. In recent years the stalemated system has become increasingly unstable as economic and social change has made it more and more obsolete. France is still seeking a political structure consonant with its modern consumer society. In the meantime, it has been outpaced economically by other European nations whose political systems have adapted more successfully to changing conditions.

In Germany, the working class (isolated from the political marketplace) formed the Social Democratic party in an attempt to gain entry to the market. When the other political sectors acted to deny that access, the party responded by centralizing power within its own structure and requiring the obedience of its members in an attempt to become strong enough to force concessions from the other sectors. Thus the workers' party became as authoritarian as the prevailing German political culture and as influenced by traditional Prussian values of conservatism and nationalism as was the rest of the society. Only the complete collapse of the German government after World War II provided the Germans with an opportunity to build a new political culture. The German citizen was to be transformed from someone who merely accepted government policy into an active participant willing to voice criticism and demands. The current Federal Republic of Germany (West Germany) is the longest-lasting German experiment in democracy to date, but the older citizens still do not take full advantage of their opportunities for an active role in the political system. The younger generations, however, appear to have learned the rewards of participation.

In Great Britain, as in Germany, the widening of political access and the lowering of costs occurred through changes granted by those in control of the political system—rather than through a violent destruction of the old system, as in France. However, the English aristocracy—unlike that in Germany—refrained from imposing its values upon the system or prejudicing the structure against the interests of the lower classes. A working-class party does exist in Great Britain. When this Labor party has obtained office, it has restructured the distribution of economic and social advantages to the benefit of the working classes. However, the Labor party has not been isolated or suppressed like its German counterpart, and therefore it does not command the strong voter loyalty given by German workers to their party. Fully a third of the working class in Britain typically votes for the Conservative party, whose programs generally favor the interests of the upper classes.

Because the British working class obtained relatively easy access into the political marketplace, the lower-class citizens did not develop a tradition of antisystemic actions or attitudes. Instead, they were acculturated to compromise, gradualism, and the legitimacy of competitive bargaining in the political market. During the nineteenth and early twentieth centuries, the process of political bargaining and compromise led to considerable softening of the differences between the programs advocated by the Labor and Conservative parties. Although the modern parties remain more class-oriented than those of the United States, they have moved toward a structure of multi-class coalitions (like the American parties) and away from the extreme class orientation of the French and German parties. To some extent, it appears that the earlier compromises have led to the creation of a political system so stable that it is having difficulty adapting to the socioeconomic demands of the late twentieth century.

In the United States, citizens of lower status perceive political action as quite costly in relation to the small, indirect, and uncertain benefits that it may bring. The American party system is dominated by (and responsive to) the middle and upper classes. Americans of the lower classes tend to direct their resources toward groups and activities outside the political system. Large segments of the poor have been socially, politically, and geographically isolated and, in the case of many minority groups, suppressed in their attempts to organize. Occasional outbursts of antisystemic activity by lower-class citizens are usually smothered when the major-party coalitions offer just enough benefits to outweigh the high costs of violent action against the system. The benefits offered include programs claimed to benefit the lower classes and the granting of high status to some individuals from the dissatisfied groups (for example, the appointment of a few blacks to high government positions). However, the superficial nature of these benefits is made clear by the fact that the poorest 40 percent of American families received 16.5 percent of the society's total income in 1950 and an only-slightly-improved 17.5 percent in 1970. In fact, this percentage has been decreasing since it peaked at 18.1 percent in 1968.

It is not surprising that the lower-income citizen in the United States perceives little value in casting a vote for one or the other of the major parties. He can gain more immediate benefits by devoting his resources to nonpolitical activities. If he becomes too dissatisfied with his lot, he knows that violent action or other antisystemic activity is likely to bring offered benefits from both parties, while a vote cast in an election is unlikely to bring any perceptible change in his circumstances. In contrast, the lower-income citizen in Germany, France, or Britain perceives the outcome of elections as very relevant to his own position in the society. He is likely to vote because he knows that he can cast his vote for a party that has a chance of winning power and that will deliver significant benefits to him if it does win power.

Finally, we can examine the effects that the structure of the political system has on voter participation in each of these four nations. We have discussed in earlier chapters the high organizational, legal, and institutional costs associated with effective political action in America. The greater political participation of lower-income citizens in the three European countries suggests that lower costs may be associated with political activity in those systems. The existence of political parties offering programs geared to the interests of the lower classes seems to help lower the costs of effective participation. In the United States, a voter must devote significant resources to a thorough investigation in order to decide with some confidence which party or candidate is likely to deliver more benefits if elected. In Britain, France, or Germany, however, the worker can feel quite confident that a victory by the worker's party will lead to benefits considerably greater than those he can expect if an opposing party wins the election. His investment in gathering information can be very small. Political participation beyond voting is encouraged because a person of relatively low status has a reasonable hope of attaining significant power within a working-class party organization. In the United States, however, a person of low status views his resources as inadequate to meet the high costs of attaining power within one of the major parties.

The available evidence suggests that party identification is less common in the European countries than it is in the United States. The typical European voter seems quite willing to support any party that espouses his socioeconomic interests. This evidence seems to confirm that information costs are lower in the European political structures, enabling the voter to determine fairly readily the candidate or party that offers the best bargain for him. The costs of more active entry into the political system may also be lower in the European countries, so that the citizen finds it relatively easy to move from one party into another and to make his influence felt in the new organization. Obviously, a complete analysis of voter participation in these societies would require a more extensive investigation of stratification systems and organizational structures along with the general concept of political culture that we have used as the basis for our discussion.

INDUSTRIAL NONCOMPETITIVE SYSTEMS

The noncompetitive political system resembles an economic marketplace dominated by a monopoly. In such a political system, all political resources such as power, status, and wealth are controlled by one individual or one group. Political sectors (interest groups) can act (or even exist) only as the political leadership allows. Other political entrepreneurs are barred from the marketplace. The political leadership maintains its position of control by imposing very high costs (sometimes including annihilation of offending groups or individuals) upon the formation of political sectors and upon the act of political opposition to the government.

Because access to the political marketplace is strictly controlled, sectors cannot freely present their demands, nor can potential leaders compete to offer alternative policies. There can be no significant bargaining about the distribution of advantages and disadvantages in the society because even the recognized sectors are not permitted to invoke any sanctions (such as withdrawal of support or denial of resources) against the government. These recognized sectors serve only to disperse government-issued information to the citizenry and to mobilize the citizens in support of the government when demanded.

Such exchange as does occur in a noncompetitive system is severely restricted, because the government arbitrarily establishes the rules under which the exchange can be worked out, and it deals from a position of overwhelming power in any bargaining that does occur. Real demands from various sectors may be suppressed, while the government can use its domination over the information system to generate apparent demands that justify its policies. Of course, just as there are no actual perfectly competitive political systems, so there are no actual perfectly noncompetitive systems. However, it is useful to classify actual systems as more similar to one or the other of these theoretical extremes.

Here we will discuss the Soviet Union as an example of a political system that is close to the noncompetitive extreme. In our discussion of Soviet politics, we emphasize the role of information in the system and the roles played by the various political sectors that do exist. We compare the Soviet system both with the purely noncompetitive theoretical model and with the competitive systems that we have already examined.

We can easily identify four political sectors within the Soviet system: the Communist party, the governmental bureaucracy, the armed forces, and the industrial-technical specialists. (The secret police formerly acted as an important political sector, but their independence and influence has diminished greatly since the death of Stalin.) These four groups control most of the political resources in the society, with the party serving as the major sector in establishing the terms of interaction. In the bargaining among these sectors, each sector seeks to influence public policy in directions that will increase that sector's share of the society's resources and will decrease its costs. The military sector, for example, may seek greater emphasis on investments in heavy industry and weaponry; it may be forced to bargain with the specialists, who wish to invest the same resources in production of consumer goods. Similarly, the bureaucracy may use its influence to bargain for greater control over economic policy, while the specialists bargain for greater freedom of investigation and experimentation and for the priority of technical criteria over bureaucratic rules and routines.

The Communist party sometimes functions as an arbitrator of disputes among the other sectors. It also functions as a bargaining arena; groups and individuals seeking power within the party structure advocate certain positions favored by other sectors in order to obtain support from those sectors for their attempts to gain power within the party. Coalitions form around policy proposals as well as around party factions seeking power. The coalitions shift as leaders alter their positions in order to obtain support from various sectors. In the struggle for power after Lenin's death, Stalin was able to form a coalition that defeated Trotsky, in large part because of Stalin's opposition to the plan of rapid forced industrialization advocated by Trotsky. After his position of power had been firmly developed, however, Stalin reversed himself and instituted a program similar to the one he had previously opposed, successfully defending this policy against the opposition of Bukharin. After the death of Stalin, Khrushchev attained power in part because of his opposition to Malenkov's plan to devote more resources to production of consumer goods. A few years later, Khruschev reversed his position and supported a shift toward a consumer orientation. The current policy of détente with capitalist countries is advocated by Breshnev with the support of the specialist sector, apparently against the opposition of segments of the military, who fear a decline in their ability to command resources for the armed services.

The political exchange in the Soviet Union differs from that in competitive systems by its exclusiveness, its flavor of oligopoly (domination by a few powerful sectors), and by the high costs associated with failure. In the past, individuals who failed to maintain strong political support within the leadership have often suffered death; even today, political failure often brings a severe loss of status, prestige, and power.

Organized groups other than the four sectors we have identified do exist within the Soviet Union. However, these groups (such as trade unions) lack autonomy and direct access to the political marketplace. These groups function in a manner quite different from that of similar groups in competitive systems. In the Soviet Union, groups do not barter for political support or make political demands on behalf of their members and mobilize their members to achieve goals established by the leaders. Their role in conveying information from the citizenry to the leadership is quite limited. The party seeks to monopolize as far as possible the key resource of political power, the ability to limit access to the political marketplace. Given the high costs of access to the Soviet political system and the citizen's limited ability to influence public policy, we might wonder how legitimacy is maintained? Of course, no political system can endure without offering its citizens a combination of rewards and threats that will win their acquiescence if not their active support.

In the Soviet Union, both material and psychological rewards are offered to the factory worker, the farmer, and the theoretical physicist who accept the legitimacy of the government. Neither the government nor the Communist party is content with ideological support from an elite group and mere acquiescence by the general citizenry to the leadership is quite limited. The party seeks to monopolize as far as possible the key resource of political power, the tion of Communist theories to the life of the factory, farm, party, and nation. Alienation—theoretically impossible in Soviet society—is fought practically through education, the manipulation of information flowing from the leadership to the citizenry, and the constant monitoring by the leadership of information about the behavior of the citizenry.

During the period of collectivization and forced industrialization, Stalin refined the use of coercion into the reign of terror that we associate with his name; manipulation of information played a secondary role in retaining popular support during this period. There are disadvantages to the reliance on coercion, however. It suppresses and distorts the flow of information from the populace to the government; without accurate information, the government is unable to adjust its policies to the realities of changing conditions. The productivity of coercion is low, and its cost (in terms of decreased efficiency and inappropriate policy) is high. In the end it became clear that a highly industrialized, complex society can ill afford the consequences of reliance on coercion; since the death of Stalin, control of information has played a more important role than coercion in the maintenance of popular support for the Soviet system. The decrease in coercion has produced a more open and accurate flow of information from the populace to the leadership, which in turn has led to the formation of public policies more responsive to the needs of specialists, farmers, and workers.

From the information available to outsiders, it would appear that the legitimacy of the Soviet government is recognized by a significant proportion of its citizenry. Apparently, individuals in the society perceive their benefits from the government as sufficient to outweigh their costs (including the cost of very limited access to the political marketplace). The very high costs associated with asystemic or antisystemic action also play an important role in maintaining legitimacy. Despite many difficulties, the Soviet Union has succeeded in making itself a leader among the industrialized nations of the modern world. It remains to be seen whether a highly complex modern society (with its inevitable interdependence, differentiation, and reliance on information) can maintain a restricted political marketplace and a monopoly of political power by a very few political sectors.

THE THIRD WORLD

We treat the nations of the Third World separately here because placing these countries on the competitive–noncompetitive continuum would be the least significant observation that could be made about them. What is more important and informative about these nations is the fact that each in its own way is building a political marketplace and establishing its own modes of political exchange. Our discussion here will focus on this process, which is often called modernization.

In a typical nonindustrialized nation of the Third World, the average citizen receives an annual income less than one-twentieth as large as that of an average citizen in one of the industrialized nations. The poorer nation lacks the stock of capital resources (factories, equipment, communications systems, and skilled workers) that would enable it to produce the goods and services common in the richer nations. Its culture (including the political culture) typically includes sets of values that promote behavior patterns inconsistent with those of citizens in an industrialized nation. However, modern communications are good enough, even in the Third World, to bring information to the populace about the better life of people in economically advanced areas. The citizens of the nonindustrialized nation therefore demand a better supply of goods and services from their own government—a supply more in keeping with their "fair share" of the world's resources. The political leadership can hope to meet these demands only if it is able to speed the process of development and rapidly bring the society into a state similar to that of the industrialized nations.

Today's richer nations have gradually modernized over periods of centuries. The process of modernization has included commercialization, urbanization, capitalization, and industrialization—as well as the development of a political structure and political culture compatible with their needs. The leadership of the developing nation must try to compress this process into a period of decades. The leadership must attempt to foster structural differentiation—the creation of new institutions to allocate and extract scarce resources. Simultaneously, it must try to inculcate in the general population new patterns of human behavior appropriate to the new institutions. And it must try to maintain its existence and obtain needed resources by bargaining in the world marketplace, where it must compete with the overwhelming political, economic, and military power of the richer nations.

The countries that modernized slowly enjoyed many advantages. As modernization improved agricultural productivity, farmers gradually found it profitable to move to the cities and become workers. The process of urbanization occurred slowly enough to permit the gradual development of institutions that would give the new working class a position in the political marketplace. The steady and slow movement of families from the country to the city permitted gradual acculturation to the new lifestyles and culture of the city. Advances in technology achieved by new industries fed back to continue the gradual improvement of farming techniques. Of great importance was the fact that medicine improved slowly along with other technical advances, so that the population increased gradually from a level suited to an undeveloped country to one suited to a modern industrial nation. Nor should we neglect the fact that changes in the political structure were made to meet the demands of sectors achieving new importance in the society, rather than being imposed upon a reluctant population by the government. The demands themselves altered gradually over time. And, in the world marketplace, the developing nations of a century or two ago were not forced to compete with far more powerful nations that had already completed the process of industrialization.

In the Third World, political leaders face the dual job of building modern economic and political institutions (such as credit systems and administrative agencies) needed to extract resources for further capital investment, and of providing demanded goods and services such as modern education and health care. The leaders must also attempt to alter traditional patterns of behavior by creating systems of rewards and sanctions that will induce the population to adapt to the needs of modern economic and political systems. They must cope with extreme demands from some sectors and with great reluctance to change in other sectors. They must deal with a population explosion created by the introduction of modern medical techniques; instead of a steady supply of new workers freed from farming, they are likely to find themselves struggling with food shortages. Individuals acculturated to rural life crowd the cities in search of food and income, but they are poorly equipped to fill a productive role in industry even if jobs were available for them.

The problems of leadership in the Third World are compounded by the limited supply of wealth and trained individuals—both important resources in the reconstruction of a society. Added to this difficulty is that of a scarcity of political resources. As it tries to create a new political system, the government must also create a new political culture. It has no tradition of successful performance upon which to draw support during the upheavals and inconveniences of modernization. Various political sectors are likely to withdraw their support readily if they perceive disadvantages to themselves in particular government actions. The government is often forced to turn to the use of coercion to maintain its legitimacy. In many cases, military leaders take control of the government because of their ability to administer the necessary coercion.

The scarcity of resources produces two important phenomena. First, the citizenry's demand for goods and services often exceeds the available supply; the government must suppress or deflect the excessive demands if it is not to be overthrown by antisystemic actions. Second, in the climate of scarcity, exchange relationships take on an intensity rarely found in the developed nations. Threats become a common medium of exchange, and violence becomes commonplace. To achieve its goals and to maintain order in the marketplace, the government must invest a large portion of the available resources in the mechanisms of coercion, therefore making less investment in meeting demands and further aggravating the discontent of the populace. Given the low productivity of coercion, a vicious cycle results that often leads to chronic political instability.

The new structures and behavior patterns that the government tries to create are not accepted readily by many individuals in the society. Even those who are demanding more goods and services may be unprepared to accept the changes in behavior and lifestyle that accompany modernization. The destruction of familiar institutions and ways of interacting has great psychic costs for individuals and groups—costs that may not be outweighed by the anticipated rewards of the new system. New arrangements—political, social, and economic—shift the distribution of advantages and disadvantages in the society. Some groups inevitably view these changes as threats to their well-being or to their very existence. Various sectors may have strongly differing views about the desirable methods and rates of modernization, and about the nature of the new political system that is to be created. The end result of the attempt to modernize is often a pattern of intense conflict among sectors and a disintegration of any structure in the marketplace.

The evolution of the new nation of Nigeria illustrates many of these points. Nigeria became an independent republic in 1963, after a century of government by the British. It began its independent existence wth a competitive political system, a large educated class, and a potentially wealthy economic base. Yet the new government was overthrown in a series of coups in 1966, leading to communal violence, secession of part of the nation, and a bloody civil war. The new political system collapsed, even though it had been carefully constructed during a decade of gradual transition from British to local government. This collapse was the result of traditional ambitions and fears, inflamed by a scarcity of resources.

The British colony of Nigeria had included regions inhabited by very different cultures; the political leadership of the new nation decided that their survival as a nation and their chances of economic development required the inclusion of all these different societies in the new Republic of Nigeria. The Moslem Hausa peoples of the north had a traditional, hierarchical society, a large population, and a very undeveloped economy, based largely on subsistence farming. Because of its large population, the Hausa society was willing to enter the new federation only if it was guaranteed a majority voice in the government. The Christian Ibo peoples of the south were highly educated, mobile, and much more acculturated to European ways during the British rule; the economy of the south had been more fully developed than that of the north, and much of the potential wealth of the new nation lay in the south. For most individuals, primary identification and loyalty was given to local political structures rather than to the national system that had originally been imposed by foreign conquerors. Long-standing fears and rivalries among the various local groups persisted.

The northern Hausas dominated the political marketplace of the new nation, and they used their bargaining power chiefly to oppose change. They feared economic domination by the wealthier south and destruction of their traditional society with its familiar institutions and power relationships. The southern Nigerians feared that the northerners would use their political power to alter the distribution of goods and services to the disadvantage of the south; they resented plans to use southern resources for the economic development of the north. The southerners felt that the north was stifling their plans for continued development of southern industry. Bargaining in the political marketplace soon became an intense struggle for political control, with all sides inclined to reject any possible compromise. In an apparently rigged election, the Yoruba peoples of the west joined forces with the northern Hausas to form a political coalition that would have the power to deny almost completely the demands of the south. With their chances of success in the political marketplace cut off, the southerners turned to antisystemic actions to achieve their goals. Southern army officers led a coup that resulted in the deaths of many northern and western political leaders and in the establishment of a military government controlled by southerners. Northerners then staged a countercoup, and the continued violent struggle soon led to violence between citizens of the various groups. In 1967, southern leaders proclaimed an independent Republic of Biafra, and a destructive civil war followed for the next three years. Eventually, the Biafrans were defeated (in large part by a blockade that led to widespread starvation) and a federal military government was restored, at least temporarily.

In Nigeria, for a variety of historical and cultural reasons, the demands of each group were perceived by the others as involving unacceptable costs. With no long-standing tradition of political bargaining, each sector tried to use the opportunity of independence to obtain all of its demands and therefore rejected compromise. Exchange relations degenerated into threats (or perceived threats) and counterthreats. The political leadership failed to create new institutions and patterns of behavior that could resolve the conflicts among the various sectors of the nation. Attempts by military leaders to achieve legitimacy through coercion failed. At last, the Ibos concluded, rightly or wrongly, that the benefits of the national system were outweighed by its costs, which they perceived to be their extinction as a group; they chose a secession as a risky but potentially more beneficial alternative.

With the benefit of hindsight and a distant (and perhaps oversimplified) viewpoint, we might conclude that the leaders of the competitive political regime engaged in acts that hastened if not caused the collapse of that system. In their contest for power, the leaders used as their major political resources the group loyalties of members of their own sectors and the corresponding fears and hatreds for other sectors. The outcomes of these bargains tended to reward the separatist behaviors that eventually shattered the nation. The competitive political system might have had a better chance at survival if its leaders had found ways to add costs to separatist behavior while providing new benefits associated with behavior that supported the national system.

The example of Nigeria illustrates a dilemma that is common in developing nations. When a new political system is created, both citizens and entrepreneurs enter the marketplace without past experience to temper their actions or their expectations. In a bid for a quick rise to power, entrepreneurs are apt to make unrealistic promises in their bargains for support. Citizens are apt to expect too much from the government; lacking experience with compromise in the new system and confidence that they will eventually have an influence on policy, the citizens are likely to become quickly dissatisfied and to turn to antisystemic actions. One of the strongest demands of the citizens is that for a voice in the marketplace through elections, but the leadership soon finds that elections only lead to widespread conflict and dissatisfaction. The government therefore turns to coercion in an attempt to move ahead with its program, further inflaming the dissatisfaction of the citizenry. The use of coercion requires a centralization of political and military power in the hands of a very small group of individuals. This creates an inviting target for a coup, in which some dissatisfied group tries to seize control of the coercive machinery. After the coup, the government must rely even more heavily on coercion to prevent countercoups and other antisystemic acts. As the precedent of success through antisystemic action is reinforced, it becomes ever more difficult to establish any kind of competitive political marketplace. The use of resources for coercion inhibits the provision of goods and services to the populace, fanning the flames of dissatisfaction. In view of this set of problems, it seems almost impossible that any government in a developing nation could steer a successful course between the dangers of competitive and noncompetitive systems to survive the inevitable period of political instability following a change in political systems.

Our analysis here has barely scratched the surface of the politics of development in the Third World, but it does suggest the complexity and the fragility of political systems in the developing nations. Some nations, such as Japan and the Soviet Union, did manage to catch up with the more developed nations after a late start. It is less clear whether nations still developing today—faced with problems of population increase, food shortage, and intense world competition for scarce natural resources—can close the gap that separates them from the highly developed nations. In fact, as measured by average individual income, that gap seems to be widening today.

The problems of development do not affect just the populations of the Third World nations. In the world political marketplace, where nations and groups of nations are the bargainers, a very unstable situation has been created. Power in the world marketplace is concentrated in the hands of the developed nations, but many vital natural resources are controlled by developing nations. In fact, the world situation today is not unlike that prevailing in Nigeria immediately after independence. There is a discrepancy between the distributions of political and economic power; tensions are inflamed by rivalries and distrust among different sectors in the marketplace; the demands of the various sectors far exceed the available stock of resources; attempts to create new political structures for the world marketplace (appropriate to changing conditions) encounter resistance because they involve behaviors contrary to old patterns; political leaders seek to obtain power by manipulating national loyalties and distrust of other nations. A stable world political system can be established only if the demands of the Third World nations can be met, and that can happen only if some way is found to accelerate their development.

PERMANENT REVOLUTION?

The People's Republic of China is unusual because it is often ranked among the great powers of the modern world, but it is still in the early stages of modernization. As measured by individual income of its population, China ranks among the developing nations. However, it exercises great political influence among the Third World nations and often plays an important and powerful role in the world political marketplace. In some respects, China is similar to the developing nations we have just discussed; in other respects, it is more similar to the noncompetitive political systems of the industrialized nations. It is further unusual in its ancient cultural tradition of existence as a nation, and in the achievements of that tradition over the centuries. In short, China is sufficiently unusual to warrant a separate analysis.

Our purpose here is not to examine in any detail the political, economic, and social institutions, processes, and events of post-1949 China. Rather we wish to focus on one apparently unique aspect of the People's Republic: the attempt to achieve modernization under a system and leadership apparently committed ideologically to a version of permanent revolution.

Permanent revolution is one of the major concepts of both communist and other left-wing ideologies. Put simply, permanent revolution involves a belief in and a commitment to the continuing process of radical change in human behavior and in the relationship of the individual to his social and political environment. In the Chinese context under Mao Tse-tung, permanent revolution has involved the nearly continuous mobilization of human energy— physical and ideological—for the purpose of reconstructing human behavior patterns and the culture of the society. By mobilization, we mean the process by which resources are removed from the control of smaller groups and placed under the control of larger organizational units. In China, resources have been taken from the control of families, clans, villages, and provinces and have been put under the control of the central government. The goal of permanent revolution is not the creation of some new stable political system. Rather, the goal is the creation of a political culture that gives the highest value to a continual process of revolutionary change in the society. The objective is not a particular condition, but rather the very process of becoming. From 1934 through 1949, Mao led the difficult struggle to accomplish a Communist revolution in China. He noted that the participants in the revolutionary movement were willing to make great personal sacrifices in order to achieve goals aimed at improving the general welfare of the entire population. He also noted that, after revolutions succeed, the new governments typically soon settle into structures just as rigid and imperfect as those they replaced. The distribution of advantages and disadvantages may be changed, but the search for personal wealth and power soon leads to the creation of new privileged and deprived strata in the society. The Maoist regime in China is attempting to re-create and keep alive the revolutionary psychology of struggle characteristic of the hard years before 1949; to this end, the government seeks to resurrect and maintain the intensity of those years. The episodes of cultural revolution, the Great Leap Forward, and the activities of the Red Guard are examples of attempts by the leadership to rekindle the spirit of revolution among the citizenry.

However, the goal of permanent revolution seems to be in conflict with another announced goal of the Maoist regime; the modernization of China. Certainly modernization is a revolutionary process, and it does require the mobilization of assets. However, the attempts to keep a permanent revolution alive often seem to hinder progress toward modernization. Both political revolution and political modernization involve increasing ranges of options for individuals and for the general society—indeed, the distinction between these two types of change often seems more theoretical than practical. Yet, the goals of revolution and modernization, as expressed by the present political leaders of China, appear to be in fundamental conflict. In other nations, the process of modernization has involved the creation of new reward structures that demand new forms of individual and group behavior. The new reward structure reallocates advantages to those who adapt to the new patterns of desired behavior. In general, the number of viable options open to an individual is greater in the modernized structure than it was in the previous structure, even though some of the old options are no longer viable. The concept of permanent revolution also encourages change and a widening of individual options, but in practice permanent revolution often conflicts with modernization. Modernization requires an unequal distribution of resources within the society. Resources and rewards must be allocated to those individuals who will reinvest them in the further modernization of the society—in other words, to those individuals who have adopted the desired modern patterns of behavior. These new patterns of behavior will not appear unless they are rewarded. In practice, modernization has required specialization by individuals in particular skills needed to maintain and advance a modern society. In every modern nation, these skilled specialists are rewarded with special advantages in the distribution of the society's resources. Among the goals of the Maoist permanent revolution are the avoidance of specialization, the sharing by each individual in all the tasks of the society, and the elimination of inequalities in the distribution of resources. Attempts to achieve these goals inevitably interfere with the process of modernization.

Furthermore, the frequent mobibilization of the populace for revolutionary political struggle draws a significant proportion of the available human energy away from those activities involved in modernization. The intermittent disruption of social and economic structures is counterproductive, causing a waste of scarce resources of individual energy and commitment (unless it is assumed that every individual has a boundless supply of physical and psychic commitment). The process of mobilization itself, involving a disruption of old behavior patterns, requires the use of one part of the population to oversee and to coerce (at lease psychologically) other parts. The results include conformist behavior, inequality, and a loss of incentive for investment in productive enterprises. Economists conclude that the various revolutionary campaigns have caused extensive loss and wastage of resources and have greatly retarded the economic development of the nation. The price of simultaneously pursuing modernization and permanent revolution appears to be very high; the demands of both goals upon time, energy, and physical resources must certainly outweigh the supply available to the political leadership.

Any search for an explanation of this high-cost policy must involve a study of the Chinese leadership, particularly Mao Tsetung himself. These leaders must perceive some benefits to be attained from their policies. The leadership may obtain support for itself (against competition from other potential leaders) through the tactics we have described; the shifts between goals of modernization and revolution may reflect bargaining for support from various sectors in the political marketplace. Furthermore, the leadership may obtain significant psychological rewards from its advocacy of permanent revolution; the Chinese leaders are regarded in the Third World and in the Communist bloc as major competitors with the leaders of the Soviet Union in attempting to define the theory and goals of Communism. China's status as a world power is perhaps due more to her experimentation with permanent revolution than to her achievements in economic development. Finally, the frequent resort to revolutionary movements within the society may benefit the leadership by destroying traditional patterns of behavior that persist from the ancient cultural structure and are perceived as threats to the stability of the new political culture.

For the Chinese citizen, it is difficult to see how the benefits can outweigh the costs of the current political system. The revolutionary goal of equality requires that rewards for desired behavior chiefly be given in the form of general approval from peers; rewards of an increased supply of resources or an increased political power would tend to create unequal strata within the society. The costs of participation in the system seem to include considerable psychological stress as old patterns and values are continually discarded and replaced by new ones. From the viewpoint of one acculturated to the American political system, the benefits seem small and the costs very high. We would expect the frequent mobilization and demobilization, over time, to weaken political support for the leadership and the legitimacy of all institutions, including the Communist party, the government, and the political elite. Because the revolutionary policy interferes with economic development, it seems highly probable that the government will find itself unable to meet the basic demands of the population for goods and services, again leading to a withdrawal of political support for the leadership. Finally, the very attempt to maintain constant revolutionary change implies the constant existence of instability in the political marketplace and in the political culture—instability that would seem to threaten the continued existence of the People's Republic.

It seems likely that the conflict between goals of revolution and modernization will intensify after the demise of Mao, whose policies have ensured intense competition among his potential successors. Present Chinese policies seem to rely ever more heavily upon the use of coercion, and we have noted elsewhere the instability that normally is introduced by use of that technique for obtaining political support. We would expect either that the system will eventually become unstable and collapse, or that advocates of all-out modernization will obtain power and will close the book on the permanent revolution.

SUMMARY

In Chapter 3 we discussed the process of political exchange in the United States. First we outlined the major American political institutions that comprise what we call government and discussed the various influences upon the government and public policy. Then, using the exchange model, we examined the processes of American politics to illustrate the usefulness of the model in analyzing any legislature, political executive, bureaucracy, or political party.

In Chapter 4, we turned first to a study of some political systems that share with the United States a broadly competitive structure. In this brief analysis, we did not try to repeat a detailed study of the institutions in each nation, but rather tried to relate the unique historical evolution of each nation to the resulting political culture, with particular emphasis on the political participation of the citizenry. We then discussed noncompetitive political systems, using the Soviet Union as an example. Finally, we explored the political systems of the Third World and the People's Republic of China by examining the process through which modern political systems emerge and the resulting problems facing developing nations.

Throughout these two chapters, we focused our attention on the political exchanges among individuals and groups of individuals in the national political marketplace. In Part III, we turn to an analysis of the world political system as a marketplace in which nations are the bargaining agents.

REFERENCES

Apter, David E. *Choice and the Politics of Allocation*. New Haven: Yale Univ. Press, 1971.

Azrael, Jeremy R. *Managerial Power and Soviet Politics*. Cambridge, Mass.: Harvard Univ. Press, 1966.

Beer, Samuel H. *British Politics in the Collectivist Age.* New York: Knopf, 1967.

Dahrendorf, Ralf. *Society and Democracy in Germany.* New York: Doubleday, 1967.

Di Palma, Guiseppe. *Apathy and Participation.* New York: Free Press, 1970.

Hoffman, Stanley. "Paradoxes of the French political community." In *In Search of France,* by Stanley Hoffman et al. New York: Harper Torchbooks, 1963.

Moore, Barrington, Jr. *Social Origins of Dictatorship and Democracy.* Boston: Beacon Cass, 1966.

Nelson, Robert, and Howard Wolpe (eds.). *Nigeria: Modernization and the Politics of Communication.* East Lansing: Michigan State Univ. Press, 1971.

Okpaku, Joseph (ed.). *Nigeria: Dilemma of Nationhood.* Westport, Conn.: Greenwood, 1972.

Ploss, Sidney. *Conflict and Decision-making in Soviet Russia.* Princeton, N.J.: Princeton Univ. Press, 1965.

Shively, W. Phillips. "Voting stability and the nature of party attachments in the Weimar Republic," *American Political Science Review.* vol. 66, December 1972.

Nie, Norman H., G. Bingham Power, Jr., and Kenneth Prewitt. "Social structure and political participation: Developmental relationships," *American Political Science Review,* vol. 63, June and September 1969.

International Exchange

PART III

In the preceding chapters, we discussed interactions among individuals and groups in the national and subnational political marketplaces. In this part, we examine interactions among nation-states in the international political marketplace. Of course, decisions made by a nation are largely determined by political bargaining among individuals within the national marketplace. Such decisions are often little more than summations of interactions regarding internal (domestic) political concerns, although the personalities of national leaders are not without influence. In any case, we find it useful to apply exchange analysis to the international scene, recognizing the simplifications involved. Here we treat nations as the bargaining agents in an international marketplace, operating in an environment that includes other nations, alliance systems, and international and regional organizations.

We use exchange analysis to explore the international political system, the dynamics of alliances, and the current Soviet-American détente. Because nations do, in effect, make choices among alternatives in order to maximize the benefits (and minimize the costs) of their interactions with other nations, exchange analysis is as appropriate to the study of international politics as it is to the study of politics within the nation-state. Of course, the goods and services being bargained for are different at the different levels of analysis, as are the particular kinds of costs and benefits involved. However, because choices made by humans are basic to all levels of political interaction, political relationships at any level can be analyzed in terms of the exchange model.

We begin, in Chapter 5, with a general look at the international political system. In Chapter 6 we examine the organizations that have been created in an attempt to structure an international marketplace corresponding to that provided by the government for citizens of a single nation. Finally, we turn in Chapter 7 to an examination of the problems of war and other international exchanges involving violence or threats of violence.

International Politics 5

CHAPTER

Like a national political system, the international political system can be described as a marketplace in which various agents exchange political resources for goods and services, each seeking to maximize his own perceived profits (benefits less costs). In our application of the exchange (marketplace) model to international politics, we treat each nation as a single agent, ignoring the bargaining within the national marketplace that leads to the nation's actions and decisions.

We have seen that a stable national political system is characterized by the existence of a government to which the citizens grant legitimacy. Disputes among individuals or groups about proper public policy are resolved through bargaining within the political marketplace according to the rules and regulations established by the government. Violence or threats of violence are used only by those individuals or groups who become dissatisfied with the system and cease to grant legitimacy to the government. Violence and antisystemic action become common only during a period of instability, when no legitimate government exists or when the political culture is in a state of major transition. The international political marketplace is quite different in this respect. Threats of war are very common parts of the exchanges that take place among nations; military power often seems to be the most important of the political resources offered in international exchanges.

The pervasive threat of war in the international marketplace results from the lack of institutions where conflicting claims to scarce resources could be settled according to accepted values and rules. There is little willingness among nations to accept compromises, to believe that peaceful exchanges of resources under the rules of the marketplace will in the long run produce fair and just distributions of resources. Most important, there are few political resources other than military might (and the threat of its use) that carry value in the international marketplace. Within the American national marketplace, an individual or group can bargain with votes, money, and organizational efforts that will have important effects upon the public policy established by the government, and therefore upon the distribution of goods and services. In the international marketplace, bargaining agents recognize that votes in the United Nations seldom affect the distribution of world resources. The threat of direct and violent action is one of the few bargaining counters that carries real significance.

THE INTERNATIONAL POLITICAL SYSTEM

The international political system is the environment within which each nation makes decisions. This system is the structure of relationships among all the nations of the world—a structure that changes over time. In this section, we take a general look at the nature of the present international system, with some comments about international systems or marketplaces of the past and possible systems of the future.

A nation entering the international marketplace seeks to obtain various goods and services that it cannot efficiently provide for its own citizens from its own resources; it also seeks to obtain security from interference in its own affairs by other nations—at the extreme, security from threats to its own survival as a nation. In exchange for desired resources and security, a nation can offer its own resources of goods and services, as well as threats of violent interference with other nations. Because there is no authoritative world government to regulate interchange in the international marketplace—and because there is no political culture accepted by all nations to promote general agreement about fair and just bargains—the bargains among nations often involve escalating threats of violence that lead to international instability and frequent resorts to military conflict. At any given time in history, the international marketplace has generally been controlled by those nations or groups of nations with the greatest military power; these nations have been able to use war or the threat of war to force other nations to accept exchanges that seem unjust and unfair to the weaker nations.

Throughout the eighteenth and nineteenth centuries, the world political system was built around an oligopolistic marketplace. A small number of nations (but more than two) were able to make most of the important decisions about resource distribution through agreements among themselves; weaker nations had little bargaining power in the market. The major European nations competed for control over weaker nations, particularly those of Africa, Asia, and the Americas. Lacking any effective bargaining power in the marketplace, these weaker nations were forced to accept very unfavorable bargains in their exchanges of resources with the major powers—and often were forced even to let major powers take over control of their national marketplaces. In many cases, the offer to submit to control by a major power was the only bargaining resource available to a minor nation; even this resource was not too great, because the major power always possessed the countering threat of taking what it wanted through its superior military strength.

In bargaining among the major powers, exchanges involved economic resources, political and military support, and threats of war. The oligopolistic system seldom remained stable for very long; some major power was always willing to accept the costs of war in order to seek a bigger share of the world's resources. The concept of a "balance of power" among the major nations was popularized by the Austrian statesman Prince Metternich early in the nineteenth century. This concept involves the maintenance of a stable system through the efforts of all major nations to maintain the status quo in the marketplace. If each major power refrains from trying to alter the balance of power (that is, refrains from efforts to enhance its own strength at the expense of other major nations), it can maintain its present share of the world's resources and can join with the other major powers in keeping other nations from gaining access to the marketplace. Under this doctrine of balance of powers, for example, the major powers of the early nineteenth century supported one another in suppressing revolutions against governments of the major powers, rather than supporting the revolutionaries in an effort to gain power at the expense of the government being opposed by the revolutionary movement.

However, even though Metternich's views attained some support, the balance of power was seldom maintained for long. Bargains between major powers normally involved military threats; the formation of alliances and the stockpiling of military might were used to give credence to these threats. Sooner or later, some major power would see an opportunity to actually use its military might to obtain territory or resources from another major power—or would act because it was convinced that the other power was about to strike first. The historical record is quite clear; the oligopolistic world marketplace was unstable, with a tendency to degenerate into war among major powers after not more than a decade or two of peaceful interchange.

The oligopolistic market continued to exist during the first half of the twentieth century, although the cast of major powers changed somewhat. As a result of wars, continuing modernization in non-European nations, and shifts in economic strength as industrial and technological developments gave new importance to certain natural resources—as a result of these changes, some former major powers declined in strength and some new major powers (including the United States and Japan) gained important roles in the marketplace. The oligopolistic system remained unstable. The major powers at the beginning of the century were loosely allied in two competing groups: the Triple Alliance (Germany, Austria, and Italy) and the Triple Entente (Great Britain, France, and Russia). A sequence of international crises and regional wars led finally to the outbreak of "the great war" in 1914—all of the great national powers entered into a violent conflict larger than any in history. Apparently no nation really desired this war, but each was willing to resort to war rather than accept bargaining terms that it regarded as unfair.

After the war, the world marketplace remained oligopolistic, but with a new balance of power. Germany and Austria were greatly weakened by their defeat in the war. The new Communist government in Russia was concerned largely with its own internal political problems and with the acceleration of industrial development. Great Britain and France suffered severe economic damage during the war, and their recovery was hampered by continuing instability in their national political systems. The United States and Japan, relatively unscathed by the fighting and with their industrial development greatly speeded by the war effort, emerged as the strongest powers in the postwar world.

The government of the Soviet Union called for workers in other countries to carry out their own communist revolutions. A fascist government led by Benito Mussolini took power in Italy. As crises continued to shake the world system—particularly a series of severe economic depressions in Europe and America—attempts to establish a stable balance of power among the major powers repeatedly failed under the pressure of rapid changes in the world marketplace. In the 1930s, the Nazi government took control of Germany and soon made that nation by far the strongest military power in Europe. The fascist governments of Italy and Germany used the fear of communist revolutions and the threat of their growing military power to attain very strong positions in the world system. The militarist government of Japan similarly extended its power in Asia. The Soviet Union, with borders in both Europe and Asia, opposed the European fascists and the Japanese. Great Britain and France tried to steer a middle course, giving some support to the development of the fascist powers in hopes that they would become strong enough to balance the Soviet Union. These liberal democratic nations hoped that the fascists and communists would at best destroy each other, or at least stalemate each other in the world marketplace. The United States tried to avoid involvement in potential conflicts, hoping to avoid being drawn into another major European war.

The unstable structure of the world marketplace finally collapsed in 1939, when Germany and the Soviet Union announced the signing of a nonaggression pact that included an unannounced agreement for the division of eastern Europe between these two powers. When Germany invaded Poland in September 1939, Great Britain and France honored their bargains with the Polish government by declaring war against Germany. The war rapidly expanded to include most nations of the world and fighting over a large part of the globe; this was truly a "world war" on a scale that even dwarfed the great war of 1914 to 1918, which had been confined largely to Europe. By 1942, the war involved the Axis powers (Germany, Italy, and Japan) against the Allied powers (Great Britain, the United States, and the Soviet Union—which had joined the Western powers after a surprise attack by Germany in 1941).

After the war, a new situation developed in the world marketplace. Germany, Italy, and Japan were thoroughly defeated in the war and left with little bargaining power. The war drained the economic resources and manpower of Great Britain, leaving that nation severely weakened. France had been overrun by Germany early in the war and suffered great destruction during the conflict, leaving France a major power in name only. Because of the role played by Chinese armies in the battle with Japan, China was given formal recognition as one of the major Allied powers; however, China was so little developed industrially that it played a relatively minor role in the postwar marketplace.

Only the Soviet Union and the United States emerged from the war with both military and economic strength. These two nations were so much stronger than any others that no other nation or group of nations could bargain as an approximate equal with either of them. In the resulting duopolistic marketplace, the two superpowers competed with each other to determine the distribution of the world's resources. Other nations were forced to seek what advantages they could obtain by offering their loyalty to one superpower or the other. If a weaker nation tried to use the threat of shifting its loyalty as a bargaining resource, it risked becoming the site of a regional war in which the two superpowers would participate indirectly while avoiding direct military confrontation.

In retrospect, the duopolistic marketplace seems to have been remarkably stable. In the oligopolistic system, there had seldom been a decade without at least one war between major powers; but the duopolistic system prevailed for more than two decades without a direct military confrontation between the two superpowers. In large part, this stability existed because nuclear weaponry gave each superpower the ability to annihilate the other, even after enduring a surprise attack. Thus, neither superpower could risk direct war against the other without inviting its own destruction. Instead, the superpowers waged indirect struggle through their support for minor powers engaged in regional or civil wars; the continual threat that these local conflicts might flare up into direct war between the superpowers kept the world marketplace in a nearly constant state of crisis. Thus the costs of stability in the duopolistic market included a competitive arms race, periodic international crises, and guerilla wars waged in geographic areas far from the home bases of the superpowers.

Today the world marketplace is evolving toward what some writers have called a multipolar system. The United States and the

Soviet Union remain by far the strongest military powers; no alliance of nations can be formed that would be able to eliminate either of these powers without a serious risk of nuclear destruction. However, Germany and Japan have recovered from the war and have become economic powers able to bargain almost as equals with the USA and the USSR. Several nations are developing their own capabilities to use nuclear weapons. Thus, some powers do exist that can exert strong bargaining power against the former superpowers.

The modern world marketplace resembles the oligopolistic marketplace of the period before World War II, but the inequalities among nations are greater in the current market (both among the major powers and between them and the minor powers) and the costs of entry to the marketplace are much higher.

Five powers dominate the current world market: the United States, the Soviet Union, the People's Republic of China, Japan, and the emerging coalition of nations in western Europe. China has emerged as a major power chiefly because of success in seeking bargains from both the Soviet Union and the United States, as each seeks to prevent the firm alliance of China with the other. There is intense competition among these five powers—and between them and the other nations and groups of nations—for goods, scarce resources, and political support.

Any analysis of the current market is, of course, tentative. The structure of advantages and disadvantages and the nature of rewards and sanctions in the new multipolar market are still undefined. Although the former superpowers no longer control the market as completely as they did a decade or two ago, they still dominate the other major powers. Japan lacks a modern military capacity; China remains economically underdeveloped, even though it has attained nuclear capabilities that give it some military strength; the western European coalition exists as a significant military and political power only in blueprint form. It is possible that Japan, China, and western Europe will overcome these disadvantages and achieve positions of bargaining equality with the United States and the Soviet Union. In that case, a new oligopolistic marketplace will be created. It remains to be seen whether the existence of nuclear weapons will enhance the stability of such a marketplace.

Other possible transformations of the international system should be considered. If even the smallest nations eventually acquire nuclear weapons, the resulting military threat might make it possible for every nation to enter the world marketplace on roughly equal terms with every other nation. Each nation would be capable of making the ultimate threat to the survival of any other, so that other political resources might become relatively unimportant. It is not easy to determine whether such a marketplace of "perfect" competition would be stable or unstable. Like the duopolistic marketplace of the postwar decades, it might prove to be a relatively stable "balance of terror" in which direct conflicts would be avoided. On the other hand, minor conflicts might incite a spiralling disequilibrium leading to worldwide nuclear war.

Another possible international market is the pure monopoly where there is only one power—a world government. Such a monopoly might result through another major war from which only one nation emerges with overwhelming power, or through the desire of all nation-states to unite under a worldwide government. With such a monopolistic system, the world political marketplace would become very similar to present national marketplaces; international politics would become similar to present national politics, and the prevalence of war as an instrument of national bargaining would presumably be ended.

Several other aspects of the international system are relevant to our discussion of exchange among nations. A national government seeks to maximize the security and the well-being of its citizens—or of those sectors that hold political power in the national marketplace. Therefore, a nation will compete in an international marketplace only if it perceives the structure of the marketplace as favorable to its own interests. Those nations who profit from an existing international system are unlikely to desire any change; those who feel that they exert little influence in the marketplace will attempt to alter the rules or to establish a new system. Because no legitimate world government exists to regulate change and competition, nations frequently resort to unilateral actions that create instability. Nations benefiting from the existing structure perceive these actions as threats to their security and well-being. Major powers may collaborate to some extent in attempting to quell such threats to the existing system, but at the same time they normally try to use these instabilities as bargaining leverage in attempts to enhance their own status in relation to one another.

Exchanges in the world marketplace often involve certain goods or services being traded for other goods and services. They also often involve goods or services being traded for political concessions that may bring security or enhanced status in the world market.

Some nations are favorably situated as major suppliers of desired goods—for example, the Arab countries with respect to oil, or the United States with respect to agricultural goods. These nations may be in a position to impose a high cost (in goods and services) on others, or to demand political concessions that significantly alter the structure of the world marketplace in their own favor. The resulting imbalance in distribution of resources may generate instability and invite reprisals. Threats of direct action and promises of political support are the most important items traded in the international marketplace: threats to punish militarily or to withhold desired rewards and goods; promises to give military or political support in various international exchanges, or to deliver desired resources.

Perceptions play an important role in international politics. If there is a widespread expectation of imminent war, any national government is likely to be very ready to interpret the actions of other states as threats to its own security. Competition is intensified when a country views gains for some other nation as losses for itself. The intense competition between the United States and the Soviet Union after World War II is an example of such a situation; each of the superpowers felt that any success by the other must be regarded as a setback for its own interests. An apparently endless armaments race for military supremacy was one of the results. The goal of national security is an elusive one; security is always relative. The Cold War arms race led eventually to a search for security in a mutual ability to achieve complete annihilation of the other superpower, no matter which superpower attacked first—in short, in the capacity for mutual suicide. The search for security only assured continued feelings of insecurity, since neither side could ever be sure that the other would not be insane enough to launch an attack—or that the other side might not have achieved a secret breakthrough that would enable it to survive (or expect to survive) the holocaust of nuclear war.

An unwillingness to compromise seems inevitable in a marketplace that lacks a regulating authority which participants can trust to achieve a generally just distribution of resources over the long run. Because no nation can feel that its security is guaranteed by the system, each nation is likely to risk high costs by taking direct action when it sees a chance to gain some important benefit. In recent years, it has become clear that the world's resources of coal, oil, and certain other mineral resources are very limited. The present industrial powers achieved modernization through liberal use of these resources, and they continue to consume them at a profligate rate.

Other nations now demand a share of these resources to support their own modernization, while the industrialized nations seek even more resources to support continued growth. The growing recognition that the supply of resources is completely inadequate to meet the demand lends desperation to the bargaining efforts of all nations. The instability in the marketplace is further heightened by the glaring inequalities of rewards, costs, and access to the marketplace where power (the ability to minimize costs and maximize rewards) is so dramatically concentrated in a few nations. The weaker nations—with the inequalities of the system constantly brought to their attention through improved world communications—are willing to take very high risks in their efforts to achieve a more just system. These nations are apt to feel that they have little to lose and everything to gain by causing the existing system to collapse.

Finally, we must discuss the role of ideological conflict in the current world marketplace. Ideological conflict is not a new feature of the international system. Conflicts between Christians and Moslems, and later between Catholics and Protestants, were very important features of the international marketplace in Europe over the centuries. The intense value conflicts between nations made compromise less acceptable and greatly enhanced the intensity of the religious wars that resulted when bargaining failed. Each nation tended to emphasize the ideological conflict in order to obtain greater support from its own citizens and from other nations in the marketplace. After the wave of nationalistic revolutions in the eighteenth and nineteenth centuries, a new ideological conflict emerged between the liberal democracies and the conservative monarchies. The intensity of this conflict gradually waned; by the beginning of the twentieth century, nations were likely to seek alliances based on considerations of the balance of power rather than upon ideological agreements.

However, the success of the communist revolution in Russia near the end of World War I led to a new ideological division in the world marketplace. The Communists urged workers in every nation to oppose their own governments and to work toward a new world system in which workers would hold political control. Other political sectors that held power in most nations sought to obtain support from their citizens in a struggle to preserve existing political institutions against the threat of communist revolutions. In the 1930s, the fascist governments of Italy and Germany developed their own ideologies, using the conflict with communism as an important part of their own value systems. As we have seen, the liberal democracies (including Britain, France, and the United States) opposed both the fascist and the communist ideologies, and sought to formulate their own ideology based upon democratic political structures and capitalistic economic systems.

After World War II, the struggle between the USA and USSR superpowers was converted by both sides into an ideological struggle. The Soviet Union called for support from its own citizens and from other nations in a struggle against imperialism and control of the world's resources by the upper classes. The United States and its allies emphasized the struggle against the totalitarian nature of government in communist countries and for preservation of "free competition" in political and economic marketplaces. Each superpower sought to convince individuals and nations that they must choose sides in a philosophical struggle, rather than entering the marketplace to bargain for the best deal they could get. Any political compromise with the opposing ideology was castigated as a desertion of important philosophical principles.

This intense ideological conflict, the so-called Cold War, greatly intensified the competition in the world marketplace. Common values and preferences between the opposing superpowers were downplayed or denied; opportunities for compromise and peaceful bargaining were scorned. One could argue that the arms race between the superpowers was as much a response to intellectual or philosophical insecurity as to any fear of actual military conquest. Each side felt a moral obligation to achieve and maintain a military superiority that would "prove" the superiority of its ideology. Each superpower perceived threats by the other not only as threats to its physical security but as threats to the survival of the all-important values that it defended. This ideological conflict was largely responsible for the perception by each superpower that any gain by the other was a loss to itself. And that perception in turn helped make reasonable bargaining and compromise in the marketplace very difficult. Once again, the intensity of the ideological competition seems to be waning. United States efforts to achieve some sort of peaceful relationship with China and détente with the Soviet Union represent a growing recognition of the need for compromise and peaceful bargaining in the world marketplace. However, there are some signs that a new ideological division may be developing between the values of the Third World nations and those of the developed nations.

ALLIANCES

The formation of an alliance between two or more nation-states is one of the oldest arrangements devised by political elites to ensure the security of their governments. Indeed, alliances existed before nation-states; the city-states of Greece formed alliances very similar to those formed by modern nation-states. When two nations form an alliance, they agree to cooperate toward certain goals or to offer one another mutual support in the event of conflicts with nations outside the alliance. In effect, the allied nations agree to act as a bargaining unit in certain kinds of exchanges with other nations.

Since World War II, the Soviet Union and the United States have divided the world marketplace into two major alliance systems. In Europe, for example, certain nations have joined the Warsaw Pact alliance with the Soviet Union, while other nations are allied with the United States in NATO. Increased cooperation among nations across these alliance divisions may indicate that the alliances are of decreasing importance in terms of the emerging international distribution of power and resources. However, as recently as June 1974 (in the Declaration of Ottawa), the United States government reaffirmed its commitment to the NATO alliance and its opposition to the goals of the Warsaw alliance.

A nation joins an alliance if it perceives such an action as offering a better chance for obtaining the best possible share of resources being distributed in the world marketplace. In most cases, the major resource being considered is security or military defense. The bargaining power of the alliance is greatly enhanced because its military strength is at least equal to the sum of the strengths of its members. For example, in an oligopolistic marketplace, an alliance might be able to bargain as an equal with a major power although each of the allied states individually is much weaker than the major power.

In deciding to join an alliance, a nation must weigh the benefits of an enhanced sense of security against the costs of possibly increased defense expenditures and the loss of decision-making freedom. As a member of the alliance, the nation may lose some freedom to choose when to wage war or when to remain neutral, because of its commitments to other members of the alliance. In many cases, nations join alliances to obtain certain benefits, but later renege on the terms of the agreement when they are asked to fulfill their commitments. NATO, for example, has never reached the levels of military forces agreed to by its member nations. Because the United States provides the greatest part of the military capability of the alliance, other members have found that they can obtain the benefits of security through the alliance without bearing the costs of full participation. In fact, France has chosen to withdraw from NATO because the mere existence of the alliance guarantees the benefits of American nuclear protection for France without any costs to that nation. The other NATO nations could not afford to allow any opposing force to occupy France because of its central location within the area controlled by NATO.

A nation may even be able to enjoy benefits from an alliance that it has never joined if the nonmember is so strategically situated as to be of importance to the members of the alliance. Such a spillover effect is a positive externality of the alliance agreement. Other externalities may be negative, imposing costs on nonmembers of the alliance. For example, consider the effects of the SEATO alliance on the strong rivalry between Pakistan and India. As a member of the SEATO alliance, Pakistan receives economic support and military supplies from its ally, the United States. Because India fears that Pakistan will use any military superiority against India, the Indian government feels obliged to invest scarce resources in defense expenditures in order to maintain a sense of security.

Alliances differ in the nature of the relationships that exist among the allied nations. The major exchange upon which any alliance is founded is the trade of decision-making options for an enhanced sense of security. However, the relative distribution of costs and benefits and the scope of choice enjoyed by the members vary greatly among different alliances. With NATO, SEATO, the Warsaw Pact, and other similar alliances of the modern world, there is one superpower that bears the major share of the economic burden of the alliance's defense system. The other members of the alliance obtain equal benefits in terms of security at much smaller economic cost. However, the superpowers are willing to accept the bargain because they are given a disproportionate voice in making decisions for the alliance. The United States and the Soviet Union have been able to act unilaterally in many situations, while their allies were able to exert little influence upon the decisions—even though the allied nations would certainly become involved if the acts of the superpowers led to war. For example, in the Cuban missile crisis of 1962, both the Soviet Union and the United States engaged in actions that brought serious risk of a worldwide war. Allies of both superpowers found themselves not only lacking a voice in the decisions taken for their alliances, but often even unaware of the decisions at the time they were made. On the other hand, when Britain and France sought to prevent Egypt's nationalization of the Suez Canal in 1956, they were forced to abandon their military efforts because the United States withheld its support for the action. The current efforts toward détente between the Soviet Union and the United States provide another illustration of the inequality of decision-making power in these alliances; apparently both superpowers have acted with very little consultation with their allies.

The Warsaw Pact and NATO alliances provide an interesting contrast in terms of the nature of relationships within the alliances. Although the nations of western Europe have not been able to obtain United States support for decisions that are opposed by the superpower of the NATO alliance, these nations have been able to take some independent actions against United States opposition and to express disagreement with United States policies. The nations of the Warsaw Pact have been much more circumspect in their disagreements with the Soviet Union; the invasion of Czechoslovakia by Russian troops in 1968 demonstrated emphatically that the Soviet Union would not tolerate open dissension among its allies. The Soviet Union holds a near monopoly over decision-making within the Warsaw alliance and has used eastern Europe as a source of scarce resources, tying the Warsaw nations economically into the Russian system. In contrast, the United States dominates NATO decision-making but has no monopoly, and the nations of western Europe have formed an economic union that has become a major competitor of the United States.

For the United States, the costs of the alliance system often appear to outweigh its benefits. The alliance system was created during the Cold War, when America felt it necessary to oppose any communist gains anywhere in the world; today the system seems somewhat outmoded. Given the military capabilities of the United States, the resources of NATO and SEATO seem to add little to American security; on the other hand, the United States is committed to the support of its allies and to the cost of maintaining their security. These commitments sometimes foreclose options for the United States or require actions that have negative consequences for the more powerful nation. For example, the United States has alienated Third World nations by supporting (with military or political backing) its European allies in their colonial policies and wars.

In some cases, the United States has found its options greatly limited by its commitments to weaker allies. In Vietnam, for example, the United States found itself in the awkward position of supporting a government while opposing many of its policies. Because the United States had committed its prestige to the support of the South Vietnamese government, it did not feel able to admit publicly that many of the actions of that government were unacceptable to the United States. The South Vietnamese government took advantage of this situation to pursue its own policies while obtaining many benefits from American support.

At the time the alliance system was created, its costs seemed reasonable in view of the need to oppose the Soviet Union in the duopolistic world market. Now that the marketplace is evolving toward a multipolar system, the costs of the alliances often seem to outweigh their benefits. The moves toward peaceful relationships with China and détente with the Soviet Union may represent first steps toward the establishment of new relationships that will eliminate the need to bear the costs of the alliance system.

DÉTENTE: A STRUCTURE FOR WORLD PEACE?

In international politics, détente means a relaxation of tensions. Today the term is used to refer to the efforts of the Soviet Union and the United States to explore new modes of interaction, to diminish the intensity of their ideological competition, and to adapt their policy objectives to the increasingly multipolar world marketplace.

This change in the national behavior of the United States and the Soviet Union may be partly attributed to the heavy costs borne by both countries in their duopolistic competition. Within each nation, moves toward détente are supported by political sectors that expect to benefit from a reduction of the amount of resources devoted to competition with the other nation. Similarly, moves toward détente are opposed by sectors that have benefited by the competition—for example, by military and industrial sectors that have gained power through the arms race. Opposition to détente also comes from those individuals and groups who accept the values and fears emphasized during the ideological conflict between the superpowers after World War II.

In the United States, the heavy cost of the Vietnam War to many sectors of the population has been an important factor in the increased desire for détente. In the Soviet Union, an important motivation for détente has been the desire to shift more resources into modernization and industrial development. Business leaders in the United States are eager to obtain access to communist populations as potential markets for their products. The leaders guiding development in the Soviet Union are eager to obtain access to Western technology. The emergence of other major powers in the world market has made the intense duopolistic competition of the superpowers seem less realistic and less desirable to many sectors in both nations. It has become increasingly clear on both sides that neither pure communism nor pure capitalism is likely to prove successful as a worldwide system. In short, more and more sectors in both nations have come to recognize that some form of compromise is necessary—perhaps even desirable.

Responding to these shifts within the national political marketplaces, the leaders of the Soviet Union and the United States have begun to seek ways to decrease the costs of competition and to establish more rewarding relationships and patterns of behavior. If the initial moves toward détente are perceived as beneficial by important political sectors within both nations, then the national leaders will obtain political support to continue investing effort and resources in the development and maintenance of détente.

The primary benefits to be expected from détente are reduced military expenditures (with a corresponding increase in resources available for other purposes), enhanced feelings of security, and increased opportunities for beneficial exchanges between the two superpowers. One important cost may be the disintegration or irrelevance of long-standing alliances. As yet, none of these costs or benefits has been fully realized. The results of the Strategic Arms Limitation Talks have not yet been reflected in reduced military budgets; important political sectors in both nations remain very insecure about the intentions of the other side; exchanges between the nations have been limited and tentative and—as in the case of recent wheat sales—have sometimes seemed to increase tensions rather than reduce them. At present it seems very difficult to tell whether the leaders of the two nations will be able to maintain domestic political support for further moves toward détente.

The impact of détente extends beyond the populations of the United States and the Soviet Union; détente involves important externalities for other nations. Some nations of western Europe, for example, have opposed détente because they fear the loss of American military protection. The Chinese government has expressed fears that détente may lead to Soviet–American cooperation in actions against China. On the other hand, positive externalities could result for many nations if détente proves successful. Soviet and American cooperation in resolving disputes around the world and in giving aid to developing nations could reduce the costs and dangers of war and increase the benefits for many Third World countries.

However, it is important to note that the moves toward détente are being made by the leaders of the Soviet Union and the United States; these moves are aimed at producing benefits primarily for those nations. Both nations obtain great benefits from the existing international structure, but those benefits have been threatened by the side effects of duopolistic competition and by the emerging multipolar market. To a large extent, détente represents an effort by the United States and the Soviet Union to maintain their positions of advantage under the present changing conditions in the world marketplace. The nations of the Third World are probably justified in their fear that détente may lead to unified Soviet–American efforts to deny them access to the marketplace and to prevent a more equal distribution of resources between the developed and the developing nations.

Détente must be viewed as one aspect of the evolution now occuring in the world political structure. More complex patterns of economic, political, and ideological competition are emerging as the duopolistic marketplace evolves into a multipolar system. The two superpowers today find themselves challenged by new competitors for scarce resources and for political support. The United States faces serious economic competition for markets and good from Japan and western Europe. The Soviet Union is experiencing competition for leadership in the communist movement from China and from the increasingly nationalistic countries of eastern Europe. Third World nations tend to regard the Soviet–American confrontation as irrelevant to their interests; as have-nots in the international marketplace, they are more concerned with a redistribution of world resources and political advantages. Recently, certain Third World nations have acted in economic alliances to exert power through control of supplies of scarce resources needed by the industrialized nations, thus significantly altering the distribution of wealth and political power in the world marketplace. The increasing power of international corporations, whose actions often seem to be beyond the control of any national government, represents another important change with results that cannot yet be predicted.

In short, the world political marketplace is in a state of transition and rapid change, and it is almost impossible to predict the structure that will emerge. The superpowers seem to be reaching agreement that military conflict carries costs exceeding its benefits. The high costs associated with the use of nuclear weapons have led to stalemates or concessions aimed at avoiding direct Soviet–American conflicts. Neither superpower has been willing to incur the worldwide disapproval that would follow from a use of nuclear weapons against a weaker nation that lacked such armaments, but neither superpower has been very successful in using its nonnuclear military might against smaller nations. Détente reflects the desire of the superpowers to turn away from military confrontations as a means of settling conflicts.

However, it is not yet clear whether such avoidance of military conflict will characterize the new structure of the world market. Nations of the Third World may be more willing to risk war in order to overcome their severe disadvantages in the marketplace. Regional conflicts may become more common in the absence of the danger that the local battle will be turned into a contest by proxy between the superpowers. Small nations obtaining nuclear weapons may decide to risk the survival of the world on an attempt to demand major concessions from larger nations.

It is not yet possible to determine whether future historians will regard détente as an important step toward the creation of a new and stable world political system, or simply as one of many fleeting changes that occurred during a period of unstable change accompanying the collapse of the duopolistic system.

REFERENCES

Boulding, Kenneth E. *Conflict and Defense: A General Theory.* New York: Harper Torchbooks, 1963.

Kaplan, Morton A. *System and Process in International Politics.* New York: Wiley, 1964.

Russett, Bruce M. (ed.). *Economic Theories of International Politics.* Chicago: Markham, 1968.

International Organization

6

We have seen that the international political system is extremely unstable, largely because of the lack of an authoritative governmental organization that could regulate the marketplace. The need for international organization has become particularly apparent in this century, when modern technology leads to the threat that any international conflict may escalate into a worldwide war. Calls for world government have been particularly widespread immediately after major wars, when the costs of instability are starkly visible. War often leads to general recognition of the fact that costs and benefits of various behaviors cannot be predicted accurately in the unregulated international marketplace. Immediately after a war, victors and vanquished alike may support moves toward creation of a world government. Unfortunately, support for international organization often evaporates as memories of the war become fainter and as nations again begin to hope for high benefits from unregulated conflict.

After World War I, President Woodrow Wilson of the United States played a major role in the creation of the League of Nations, intended to provide "mutual guarantees of political independence and territorial integrity to great and small states alike." However, Wilson was unable to obtain support for his creation within his own national marketplace, and the United States never joined the League. The Soviet Union was excluded from the League because other nations refused to give formal recognition to its Communist government. With two of the world's major powers acting outside its regulations, the League was never able to make much progress toward creation of a stable system in the world marketplace. The League was able to settle some disputes among minor nations and to promote international cooperation in distribution of economic aid and social assistance, but it proved powerless in obtaining peaceful settlements of conflicts between major powers. Nations sought security through agreements and alliances made outside the structure of the League. In the 1930s, the fascist nations launched aggressive acts against other nations with little fear of sanctions from the League of Nations; by that time it had become clear that the League could exert no significant power against any action of a major nation. When the Allied nations finally did enter the war, they did so as a result of alliances or in response to direct attack on their own territories, not in support of the rules of the League.

THE UNITED NATIONS

As they neared victory in World War II, the Allied nations began to plan for the creation of an international structure that might prevent future world wars. They hoped to create a forum in which nations could bargain effectively to achieve their goals without resort to war; they also hoped to establish a realistic expectation of serious sanctions to be imposed upon any nation that did use war as a bargaining lever in its exchanges. In designing the structure of the United Nations, the leaders of the Allied powers tried to avoid some of the flaws that had weakened the League of Nations.

One of the basic premises in the design of the United Nations was the provision of collective security for all nations. A Security Council was formed, with permanent membership given to the five major Allied powers—the United States, the Soviet Union, France, Britain, and China. If any nation attempted to use aggression against another, the collective strength of these great powers could be used to threaten or impose sanctions against the belligerent nation. If a country considering use of war were certain that its acts would result in the concerted military opposition of the "Big Five," the country would be certain that its aggressive action would involve very heavy costs. The designers of the United Nations structure believed that these costs would be large enough (and the probability of their imposition sufficient) to outweigh any benefits that the country might expect to obtain through war.

Six nonpermanent seats on the Security Council (later increased to ten) were to be filled by nations elected by the General Assembly for two-year terms. The Council was given the power to call upon member nations for military forces to be used in imposing sanctions; such action could be taken only upon the agreement of all five permanent members and at least two of the nonpermanent members. In effect, this arrangement gave each of the "Big Five" powers a veto over actions of the Security Council. The provision of this veto power should be viewed as a concession to the realities of the political marketplace. The effectiveness of the Security Council in deterring aggression depended upon the certainty that all five major powers would act together in opposing any belligerent nation. Sanctions would not be effective if one major power refused to regard the accused nation as the aggressor, or if a major power found it in its own national interest to permit the aggressive nation to proceed with its actions. In that case, the attempted imposition of sanctions would be more likely to lead to war between the major powers than to successful peacekeeping.

The existence of the veto power has proved to be a serious limitation upon the ability of the Security Council to fill its intended role. The founders of the UN apparently failed to foresee the emergence of the duopolistic market in which the United States and the Soviet Union would take opposing sides on almost every international issue. Because each of these superpowers held a veto over Security Council actions, any nation contemplating aggressive action could be reasonably sure of avoiding sanctions if it obtained the support of one of the superpowers. The ideological conflict of the Cold War created an atmosphere in which the superpowers felt it necessary to oppose one another over most regional conflicts, so the threat of Security Council sanctions became almost meaningless.

However, the Security Council has functioned as a stabilizing influence in the world marketplace, despite the failure to impose effective sanctions on belligerent nations. Nations involved in disputes have often found it worthwhile to bring their problems to the Security Council for debate and discussion. Each nation hopes that the public discussion of the issues will lead other nations to support its position. Even if it expects a veto to prevent direct Security Council action in its favor, the nation may hope to obtain a majority of votes in the Council, thus winning prestige and vindication in the international marketplace—rewards that can in turn be used as political resources in the dispute.

The face-to-face interactions in the Security Council have sometimes led to the achievement of a peaceful compromise between the disputants. In many cases, the positions taken by major nations during the debate permit the conflicting nations to obtain a clearer estimate of the probable costs and benefits of a war as they become more able to predict the support that other nations will give to each side if a war does begin. One nation may recognize that war would involve unacceptable costs; acquiescence in a decision by the Security Council provides a relatively low-cost, face-saving alternative to continuation of the conflict. In addition, use of the veto power often served as a signal between the superpowers that a given issue was considered too significant to permit public compromise. Therefore, a veto by a major power often led to private negotiations over the issue. At worst, one side was able to use limited war to achieve its ends, while the other side had to be satisfied with a hot debate and a face-saving majority vote at the council table.

The existence of the veto power spared the major powers the embarrassment of defying the United Nations structure rather than compromising their perceived vital interests in certain issues. Because no nation would be likely to accept a decision that it viewed as seriously damaging to its own interests, the lack of a veto power would almost certainly have led various major powers to act against the forces of the United Nations in certain conflicts. Such actions in turn would probably have led to the complete collapse of the Security Council as a significant factor in the world marketplace. The Soviet Union, for example, often impeded use of sanctions against belligerent nations through the use of its veto. However, it can be argued that this result was far preferable to a situation where the Soviet Union would have felt compelled to withdraw from the United Nations to express its opposition to decisions taken by a majority of Council members; it seems likely that the UN would have become as ineffective as the earlier League of Nations if one of the superpowers had been excluded from its structure.

The record of the Security Council is one of mixed success and failure in promoting peaceful settlements of disputes. In disputes that involve vital interests of a superpower, the Security Council has failed to contribute much toward peaceful resolution of the conflict. For example, the dispute between the United States and the Soviet Union over rights of access to Berlin was settled through displays of military strength and through private negotiations after the Security Council proved unable to settle the dispute. In disputes that do not directly involve vital interests of the superpowers, the Security Council has often been able to play a meaningful role in achieving solutions. In the 1965 conflict between India and Pakistan over control of Kashmir, for example, the Security Council was able to arrange for mediation of the dispute, even though the Council was unable to impose a definitive solution through its own action.

Measures have been taken in many situations to circumvent the power of the Security Council and the use of the veto power in the Council. The Secretary-General of the United Nations has often carried out missions of discreet diplomacy aimed at the resolution of conflicts—a practice begun by Dag Hammarskjöld in 1965 when the veto power prevented resolution of certain conflicts in the Security Council. Many important matters of international peace and security have been transferred from the Security Council to the General Assembly. In that larger body, each member state has a vote, and no veto power exists. The enlargement of the powers of the General Assembly has permitted successful settlement of some conflicts that might have resulted in a stalemate within the Security Council. On the other hand, the Security Council has been able to use its power in a few conflicts, at least to contain a regional conflict and prevent its expansion into a wider war. The Congo crisis of 1960 provides one example in which the Security Council was able to function in more or less the manner originally intended.

A very significant change in the Security Council occurred in 1971, when the People's Republic of China was given a permanent seat on the Council. The Nationalist government of China (which for many years had held actual power only over a few offshore islands, but had retained its formal role as a major power in alliance with the United States) was expelled from the United Nations. The decision to grant communist China the role of a major power within the

Security Council was the result of a realistic reappraisal of the world balance of power. Consensus between the two superpowers was no longer sufficient to regulate the behavior of the many nations seeking and gaining additional strength in the world marketplace. The People's Republic of China, supported by many nations of the Third World, had argued that the United Nations (and its attempt to use rewards and sanctions to regulate the political marketplace) was irrelevant to the values, beliefs, and needs of the majority of the world's population. The exclusion of the People's Republic from the UN seemed to confirm this viewpoint. If the People's Republic continued to be alienated from the one structure that sought to provide guidelines for peaceful political interaction in the world marketplace, then the efforts of the United Nations would eventually have been totally doomed.

A political marketplace—especially one accommodating such a diverse group of members and potential members as the nations of the world—can remain viable only if it is based upon a shared set of expectations. These expectations will persist only if they are periodically reinforced. Should even one major agent in the market reject the shared assumptions about the rules of modern international politics and act according to a different set of rules and expectations, then even the minimal structure that exists in the market would collapse; nations would be forced to bargain in terms of military threats and acts—resources that retain their power in an anarchistic marketplace.

The General Assembly of the United Nations was designed as the great deliberative body of the organization. Because each of the 135 member states (as of 1974) has one vote in the Assembly, a lengthy and cumbersome debate normally is required to reach a decision on any matter before the Assembly. In the original General Assembly, there were only 50 votes. Because most of the original member states were allies of the United States, the Assembly could generally be expected to deliver its support to the United States position on any issue. With decolonization and the proliferation of new nations—including the so-called ministates with tiny populations and poorly developed economic systems—each casting a vote in the Assembly, it has become increasingly difficult to predict the winning coalitions on international questions. The newer and smaller states now have an opportunity to play significant roles in political bargaining in the Assembly. The major powers are forced to grant various concessions to obtain the support and votes of the smaller states in the Assembly because no major power exercises firm control over a bloc of weaker allied states large enough to deliver a reliable majority in the Assembly. The blocs that do exist vote with varying degrees of consistency and form ever-shifting coalitions. In addition to the blocs centered around the major powers, there are now blocs organized by various groups of minor nations in an effort to exert more power within the Assembly. Because a two-thirds majority must approve any major Assembly action, the bargaining among blocs sometimes results in a stalemate where no side can obtain approval for the position it desires.

The Assembly was originally conceived as primarily a forum for open communication and debate among nations. When use of the veto in the Security Council limited the effectiveness of that body, the General Assembly in 1950 adopted a resolution giving itself the power to take certain steps toward the resolution of conflicts. The creation of the United Nations Emergency Force (UNEF) to police the uneasy truce in the Middle East after the Suez crisis of 1956 is one example of peace-keeping actions taken by the General Assembly. In general, the Assembly has remained flexible in its approach to problems and willing to experiment with new techniques for solutions.

On the other hand, deliberations in the Assembly have sometimes deteriorated into empty rhetoric. The Assembly can function to focus interests and to offer opportunities for international communication, thereby reducing potential misperceptions of costs and benefits in the world market. However, its ability to act in this manner is apparently limited by its helplessness in influencing situations that fall within the domestic jurisdiction of a specific member state. For example, the General Assembly was unable to provide meaningful solutions when the Soviet Union moved into Hungary in 1956 or into Czechoslovakia in 1968, nor could it effectively resolve the issues of United States actions in Southeast Asia or colonial policies of the Republic of South Africa.

In certain areas, the creativity of the Assembly has led to significant progress in stabilizing the world marketplace. It has been able to obtain significant agreements on nuclear arms control among the major powers, for example, beginning with the Outer Space Treaty of 1967. The Assembly is not an authoritative marketplace where definitive decisions are made regarding the distribution of coveted resources or the dispensation of benefits and sanctions. Rather, it provides a forum where rules can be developed to cover the interactions of states with different historical perspectives and diverse political cultures. The more effective the Assembly becomes in areas of international concern, the more likely will be the reinforcement and eventual legitimization of a stable world political culture. Given the present strength of nationalistic passions, one cannot expect the General Assembly—through debate, vote, and building of coalitions—to deter a strong nation from pursuing a policy that it perceives as likely to bring desired results at an acceptable price. Strong nations will submit to international regulations only after they come to perceive even greater long-range benefits to be obtained from the functioning of a stable international government.

The founders of the United Nations created the Economic and Social Council (ECOSOC) in an effort to narrow the economic gap between rich and poor nations; the council was expected to engender and reinforce a stable political culture in matters related to economic and social development. The founders hoped that a start toward international order could be made in this concrete domain—an area that seemed at the time to be relatively free from sensitive political conflict among major powers. They felt that it would be possible to produce beneficial results for the developing nations through supplying some of their basic requirements for scarce resources; at the same time, the wealthier nations would come to realize that their national interests were helped rather than harmed by their cooperation with the decisions of this United Nations body. Thus, both rich and poor nations would be reinforced for their cooperation with the international organization, and the United Nations would gain legitimacy in the eyes of all member states. Norms of behavior appropriate to a world political culture would be created and strengthed through ECOSOC actions and hopefully would later be extended to more sensitive issues among nations.

The original ECOSOC was comprised of 18 members (the membership was increased to 27 nations in 1966). The member states (elected by the General Assembly for three-year terms) unofficially reflect the power configurations within the Assembly and always include the permanent members of the Security Council. Programs operated by ECOSOC include the United Nations Children's Fund (UNICEF) and the United Nations Development Program. Because the United States has always contributed the largest share of the budget for ECOSOC programs, it has demanded a strong voice in controlling those programs. The United States Congress must approve all allocations of American funds to support the UN budget, so the

Congress has been able to exert strong bargaining power in determining ECOSOC policies through its threats (sometimes explicit, more often implied) to refuse to fund the council. During the Cold War, the United States often was able to stalemate UN programs that were perceived as detrimental to American interests in the duopolistic competition. Détente between the superpowers has been reflected in the present UN policy of giving nonpolitical aid to nations in economic need. Recently, a coalition of Arab, Third World, and communist member states has acted as a relatively powerful bloc in the General Assembly, and this bloc has also begun to exert strong political influence on ECOSOC policies and programs.

In two new United Nations bodies created during the 1960s— the Conference on Trade and Development (UNCTAD) and the Industrial Development Organization (UNIDO)—there has been an interesting shift in the positions of the superpowers. Initially, the United States and the Soviet Union competed to win the favor of various developing nations by offering various benefits in return for political support. More recently, the superpowers seem to be acting in cooperation to resist increasing demands upon their wealth and resources made by the less developed nations. In this and other examples discussed earlier, we see that political bargaining in the international marketplace carries over into the formal structure of the United Nations and even into the functioning of organizations designed to be nonpolitical. As the superpowers found it to costly to continue their competition for the favor of the many small nations, they have begun to invest energy in the search for alternative policies. However one may assess the desirability of these changes, it is clear that the process of bargaining—the attempt to achieve maximum benefits at minimum cost—continues despite changes in the rules and structures that regulate exchanges among nations.

Two important bodies created as part of the original United Nations structure were designed to solve international problems that might tend to disrupt the international political structure. The Trusteeship Council was formed to facilitate an orderly transition from colonialism to independence, in recognition of the fact that colonial empires were no longer worth their cost to the major powers. The council played a major role in achieving independence for most colonies, and it is phasing itself out of existence today. The other important body, the World Court, had been created as part of the League of Nations and was retained as part of the United Nations structure. The Court was intended to adjudicate legal disputes arising between nations—disputes involving legal interpretation of treaties, international agreements, and the Charter and regulations of the United Nations. It was also hoped that the World Court would become a definitive source of international law covering new areas of interaction among nations. The ability of the World Court to fulfill its tasks in view of the realities of international politics is one of the subjects of Chapter 7.

The founders of the United Nations placed the executive power for the organization in the Secretariat, headed by the Secretary-General. The Secretariat was conceived as a staff of international civil servants, chosen from among the talented and skilled individuals of all nations because of their specific expertise and not for political considerations. The Secretariat was expected to provide permanence and stability in the United Nations structure. The founders hoped that individuals within the Secretariat would regard themselves as citizens of the world, abandoning their loyalties to the nation-states from which they came.

At first, there were fears that the Secretary-General would become either an overly independent and powerful force embarrassing states as they pursued their national interests or a weak bureaucrat subject to the political whims of the major national powers. These fears have subsided as various individuals occupying the office have established the image of the Secretary-General as a competent administrator who can act as a mediator in political disputes because nations are likely to accept his suggestions as alternatives less costly than war. For the most part, the Secretariat has functioned as it was intended to do, and its staff has acquired general respect throughout the international marketplace.

The United Nations has not become for the international marketplace what a government is for a national marketplace. It lacks the authority or the legitimacy to issue authoritative decisions or to impose regular sanctions upon agents in the marketplace; it is dependent upon the voluntary acquiescence of its member states, both for financial support and for the implementation of decisions. These decisions have political ramifications that are important both to the organization and to its member states. The United Nations has become an additional channel through which nations communicate and bargain for a better position in the world marketplace. If nations continue to obtain advantages through cooperation within the structure of the United Nations and through submission to its decisions, then perhaps the organization will eventually achieve the legitimacy needed to enable it to function as a true world government. For the present, however, it functions primarily as a forum for international communication, a place where nations can make their demands known and can at least receive the satisfaction of knowing that they have been heard by representatives of the world's population.

REGIONAL EXCHANGES

The United Nations represents the most extensive and ambitious effort at international organization in the present world marketplace. In an effort to attain legitimacy as the major formal structure of the marketplace, the United Nations has granted access to nearly every state that maintains an independent existence, regardless of its size or power. As a result, the organization is often sluggish and awkward in responding to issues, because numerous factions must be heard and allowed to bargain even if they have little direct involvement in the problem under discussion. Therefore, regional organizations founded on geographic proximity have been formed to handle many issues that are crucial to these states but of less significance to others. Most of these regional organizations are composed of states linked by similar interests and political cultures.

In Chapter 5, we discussed alliances—groups of nations organized primarily to provide mutual military support. Here we are concerned with organizations created to facilitate a broader range of political exchanges among the member nations. The Organization of American States (OAS) is such an organization; it performs numerous functions, ranging from promotion of hemispheric collective security against outside nations to provision of structures for the conciliation of disputes among member states. The main body of the OAS is the Assembly of Foreign Ministers, which meets annually and has exhibited considerable flexibility in its approaches to problem-solving. The OAS is forbidden to intervene in the internal affairs of member states, and there is a considerable variety of political structures among the member nations; nonetheless, the OAS nations have demonstrated a willingness to deal with one another on many levels through the structure of the organization. The nations have come to expect substantial rewards in return for giving their support to the rules and regulations of the regional exchange. These rewards include face-saving solutions to conflicts with neighboring states and various political and military advantages. However, differences in political cultures and values placed on various types of rewards remain marked among the OAS nations, and there seems little tendency for the OAS to evolve toward the role of a supranational government.

The Organization of African Unity (OAU) provides another example of efforts to structure regional exchanges for members having both common interests and broad cultural differences. The OAU was created in 1963 by 31 independent African states. These nations have acted in concert in issues involving opposition to colonialism, and they have even been able to solve issues where interests of member states conflicted, as in cases of border disputes and internal conflicts. The organization has experienced problems similar to those experienced by other international structures; it remains to be seen whether the successes of the organization have provided sufficient reinforcement to cause its member nations to continue their support for further development of the regional political exchange.

Certain regional arrangements, such as the Arab League, are based primarily upon a common cultural heritage. Even within such an organization, disputes and conflicts among member states are far from infrequent. It often seems that a shared animosity toward Israel is the main influence holding the Arab League together; ironically, success in the elimination of this perceived common enemy might well lead to the collapse of the organization. Until the League can provide positive rewards for its member states in other matters, it seems unlikely to evolve into a significant marketplace for political exchange.

COMMON MARKETS

Some regional organizations are based primarily upon practical economic interests. With a minimum of shared values and assumptions, nations may be willing to give up some independence in economic matters in order to obtain the benefits that follow from the ability to act as a powerful bloc in the world economic marketplace. In the economic realm, costs and benefits can be clearly defined in terms of dollars, so that it is relatively easy for the leadership of a nation to determine with confidence the profits to be obtained by membership in such an organization—and to convince the political sectors of its national marketplace that membership is beneficial.

The European Economic Community (often called the Common

Market) is perhaps the best example of such an organization; it facilitates such actions as joint tariff regulations and envisions an eventual integration of economic efforts among member nations. The nations of the Common Market share very similar attitudes, goals, and value structures; the costs of membership in the organization are very small in comparison to the projected benefits. Still, political conflicts among member nations have impeded progress toward full economic integration of the member states. For example, France repeatedly blocked Britain's entrance into the organization until 1972. Political conflicts between France and Britain continue to hamper the actions of the organization.

To some extent, the economic success of the Common Market is providing reinforcement for behavior that supports the cooperation of the member nations. To this extent, traditional nationalistic distrusts are being weakened and a sense of European unity is being fostered among member nations and their citizens. The behavior of individual nations does appear to be tending toward the desired norm—acting as a member of a European community rather than as a potential enemy of the other European states. If this trend continues, the success of economic cooperation may lead eventually to an extension of the regional organization into other realms of international exchange. Some have gone so far as to hope for the eventual evolution of a true European government and the creation of a United States of Europe.

INTERNATIONAL NONGOVERNMENTAL ORGANIZATIONS

Thus far we have discussed international exchanges in which national governments act as the bargaining agents. However, advances in the technology of travel and communication have led to greatly increased contacts among individuals and subnational groups across national boundaries. In many cases, political sectors find it useful to cooperate with corresponding political sectors in other nations, creating international organizations that further their interests and supporting one another in efforts to influence their respective national governments. Where such nongovernmental organizations provide significant benefits to their members, the members may come to identify themselves more closely with the organization than with their own national governments. One possible direction for future evolution of the world marketplace is the strengthening of these international nongovernmental organizations and the eventual withering away of national governments. In such a case, a world political structure might be constructed directly from worldwide political sectors, rather than through the cooperation of national governments in a world government.

One of the functions of ECOSOC is to grant official UN recognition to international nongovernmental organizations. Such organizations include the International Chamber of Commerce and the International Conference of Free Trade Unions, as well as other groups dealing with such matters as education, religion, veterans' affairs, and agriculture. As yet, these organizations play relatively minor roles in the world political marketplace, but their power and significance seems to be increasing.

INTERNATIONAL CORPORATIONS

Like other aspects of the world political marketplace, the nature of business organizations and exchanges has changed drastically in recent decades. Many of these changes are the results of technological innovation and its consequences. Large business enterprises have expanded their activities around the globe; many international corporations now act as important powers in several national marketplaces and perceive their interests as quite independent of the interests of any particular nation. Certain key industries that are vital to modernization and development—such as industries involved in transportation, communication, exploitation of scarce natural resources, and energy supply—have long exerted important influence within their respective national marketplaces. Today many of these industries act as international powers, often functioning as relatively independent agents in the international marketplace.

In recent years it has become clear that these corporations often use their economic power to operate outside the rules and regulations of national marketplaces. Cases have been exposed where certain corporations regularly bribed government officials, financed political campaigns, and perhaps even arranged assassinations or supported revolutions in order to further their own interests. Many of the larger international corporations rank with the medium-sized nations as financial powers in the world marketplace. In the absence of an authoritative world government to control or regulate their activities, these corporations seem to be able to function almost as supralegal independent powers; national governments find themselves relatively powerless in dealing with the corporations because only a small portion of the activities of an international corporation falls within the jurisdiction of any one nation.

In some cases, implicit alliances have been formed between major industrial interests and groups of national governments. The Organization of Petroleum Exporting Countries (OPEC) in effect acts as an alliance between major oil corporations and the governments of oil-producing nations. Through OPEC, the national governments and the oil industry have cooperated in obtaining higher prices and profits for petroleum, especially from customers in the industrialized nations. The oil-producing nations have benefited through an unprecedented shift in the distribution of the world's wealth; within a few years, these nations have moved into the position of major financial power in the world marketplace. The oil corporations have benefited through increased profits and increased political power in national marketplaces.

On one hand, we might view international corporations and alliances such as OPEC as sinister conspiracies of powerful and selfish transnational interests that are abusing the international system by blackmailing nations for their own personal gain. On the other hand, we might view them as another example of new structures and behavior patterns emerging in the changing international marketplace, illustrating the potential for the creation of realistic transnational political sectors that will replace obsolete nationalistic political groupings.

Once again, we must conclude that the international political system is presently in a state of extensive and rapid transition. The structure and political culture that will emerge can be guessed at, but it cannot be predicted with confidence. At present, we cannot even determine with any certainty whether current changes are leading toward a more stable world marketplace or toward even greater instability and conflict.

REFERENCES

Stoessinger, John G. *The Might of Nations.* New York: Random House, 1973.

War, Subversion, and Terror: Law and Diplomacy Revisited

7 CHAPTER

We have noted that the international marketplace is characterized by the common use of military force or threats of its use in bargaining exchanges. This frequent resort to antisystemic activity makes the world political structure very unstable. It seems clear that most of the world's people would benefit from the creation of a stable world political system—one with a well-regulated marketplace in which goods and services could be distributed through peaceful bargaining exchanges. In this chapter we shall explore in more detail the sources of instability in the world marketplace, beginning with a closer look at the origin and nature of the nation-state as the bargaining agent in the market.

THE NATION-STATE

For the first few thousand years of recorded history, the world political system was dominated by great empires, each with a very powerful central government ruling over an extensive area. Although some empires endured for centuries, each eventually collapsed, and the empires eventually disappeared entirely from the world system. The ancient empires showed three major weaknesses as political organizations. First, each empire sooner or later found itself unable to supply the vast quantities of goods and services demanded by its large and farflung population and thus lost legitimacy in the eyes of its populace. Second, the process of decision-making involved very high costs due to the difficulties in moving information and resources over the great distances between the central government and the outskirts of the empire. Third, the monopolistic control of the empire over the political and economic marketplaces impeded technological innovations. With the central government in complete control of such services as communication and transportation, there was little potential benefit to encourage someone to pay the high costs of developing and introducing a new device to provide more efficient service. Slow and inefficient communication and transportation reduced the flow of information and political support to the central government, forcing it to rely largely upon coercion to maintain its power.

After the fall of the Roman Empire, the European political marketplace became fragmented, and the power of Rome was scattered among a variety of small feudal states. In part, the feudal system was characterized by a rigid social hierarchy cemented together by personal pledges of loyalty of vassals to their lords. The king, the supreme head of a kingdom, granted hereditary fiefs (control over an area of land and its people) to his vassals in return for their loyalty and military support. In general, these vassals of the king were lords of the realm who, in turn, had their own vassals to whom they granted fiefs, and so on down the line to the least powerful nobles. The church, whose influence had spread through former Roman territory, held its own fiefs, but the clergy owed loyalty to the head of Christendom, the pope, as well as to their king. High-ranking churchmen often occupied positions of great political power and were sometimes powerful enough to oppose the interests of the nobility and even the monarchs.

At the bottom of the feudal hierarchy, the vast majority of the people were hereditary serfs, dependent on nobles for their land and homes. The common people had been driven into serfdom as the Roman Empire collapsed and they found themselves without the protection of Roman law and Roman government. The later Roman and early medieval period was characterized by sudden attacks of invaders, crushing taxes, armed uprisings, and oppressive government officials. Freemen and small landowners were forced to seek the armed protection of their more powerful neighbors in return for their services and their land. The children of these free people were left poor and powerless and were forced to make the best bargain they could with the great landowners. Thus, they and the descendants of people who had been captured and enslaved by the Romans were gradually joined together in serfdom. Serfs generally owed a fixed amount of work and a fixed share of their crops to landowners in return for military protection, other benefits, and the right to live and farm on sections of land allotted to them.

The feudal system was in one sense highly unstable: there was almost constant competition among the nobility and clergy within a given kingdom as well as competition between kingdoms, with frequent resort to armed conflict to settle disputes. Nobles lived in fortified castles in order to defend themselves against attacks by other nobles. The small feudal states proved capable of generating innovation in war technology, probably because of the great benefits that could accrue to a noble who was able to defeat his rivals consistently. By the eleventh century, commerce, trade, and craft specialization had begun to flourish within the feudal system as well. These innovations contributed to the instability of the feudal system; the political system was constantly disrupted by warfare, and economic marketplaces remained small and unstable because of the constant disruption of the political system.

The feudal system suffered disadvantages because of its chronic instability and because of the inefficiency of its small units in producing and distributing goods and services. The gradual development of the nation-state involved two major changes in the system. First, power and decision-making authority were gradually shifted away from the smaller feudal units and toward the centralized marketplace of the kingdom, where larger scale of organization permitted greater efficiency. Similarly, smaller kingdoms were amalgamated into larger ones. Second, the network of personal bargains between lords and vassals became less important as more and more forms of direct interactions arose between the monarchical central government and the population. As towns developed, their populations of traders, craftsmen, and workers found themselves outside the feudal system—at first giving their loyalty to town governments, but later giving support to the kingdom in return for the advantages the central government could provide in regulating commerce and trade. The feudal system was further weakened as the nobility found it to their benefit to emancipate serfs, thus freeing the nobles of the obligation to provide goods and services for the peasantry and allowing them to collect rents from their newly freed tenants. When the central government of the kingdom was given legitimacy as regulator of the major political marketplace by most of its population—including farmers, traders, craftsmen, workers, landowners, and clergy—the nation-state had developed. This process occurred gradually over many centuries, but we can pick 1648 as an arbitrary date by which the nation-state had matured. In that year the Thirty Years War was ended by the Treaty of Westphalia, in which the various monarchies bargained as agents representing many sectors of their populations. In the terms of the treaty it is clear that the national governments were acting much like modern nation-states, with few of the feudal and religious elements that had typified earlier interactions among monarchies.

The development of the nation-state involved the creation of a new political culture that would reinforce a different set of values, beliefs, and behavior patterns appropriate to the new political system. The most significant shift in the political culture was the reinforcement given to the viewpoint that all individuals in the population of a nation are citizens of that nation, with the right to express demands for goods and services and to expect just treatment from the national government. The feudal serf was concerned only with his relationship to the noble on whose land he lived; he had no reason to bargain or interact with higher levels of the political structure, and very little reason to interact with serfs of other lords. The new national political culture encouraged people to interact with other people of similar position and outlook, and to form groups (political sectors) that could enter the national political marketplace to bargain for their demands. The new national political system and the new national political culture evolved together, each reinforcing the other's development.

The centralized administration of the nation-state was able to provide psychological and physical security for its citizens as it eliminated the warfare among feudal nobles. It used technological innovations to reduce the costs of decision-making for the larger organization, thus solving one of the problems that had plagued the ancient empires. As the national government gained control over the distribution of resources in the nation, it was able to use that control to provide rewards for those individuals whose behavior patterns were appropriate to the new political system. In particular, the national government tried to reinforce a spirit of national loyalty—encouraging each individual to think of himself primarily as a citizen of the nation. As nationalistic cultures developed, individual citizens became more willing to accept compromises in the political marketplace—to continue to support the government even when their demands were not fully met, believing that a stable national government would eventually provide the best possible share of available resources. This nationalistic loyalty gave the nation-state its greatest strength—an ability to draw upon the resources and capacities of actively participating citizens in times of crisis. The typical person living in an empire or a feudal state had little reason to care about the survival of the central government; he participated in its defense only when he was forced to do so, or when he could obtain immediate benefits by doing so. In the national political culture, strong reinforcements were given for unswerving loyalty to the national government; patriotism became a highly esteemed trait.

Of course, no national government was able to supply all the goods and services demanded by its citizens. In order to preserve its legitimacy, the government often placed great emphasis upon its success in providing physical safety for the populace. The value that a citizen placed upon this service could be enhanced by convincing the citizen that the national government was protecting him from terrible dangers posed by other nations. Thus, the new spirit of nationalism was strongly encouraged by building fear and distrust of other nations. Whenever significant political sectors threatened to oppose the government because it was not meeting their demands, the government found it useful to generate an apparent or real conflict with a neighboring nation. The discontented sectors could usually be convinced that the costs of national defeat would be higher than the costs of continued support for the existing national government. Thus, a tendency toward instability of the international system was built into the very structure of the nation-state, whose strongest resource was the nationalistic spirit of its citizens—a spirit often maintained and reinforced through international conflicts.

The citizen's sense of security involved not only protection from actual or perceived external threats, but also a commonality of culture within the nation, the use of sanctions to police behavior of all citizens so that an individual could have confidence in the behaviors to be expected from his fellow citizens, and the provision of a viable political marketplace in which each citizen could express his demands and receive some form of satisfaction. The national political system developed to meet these needs, taking somewhat different forms according to the historical and cultural peculiarities of each nation. The domestic aspects of national political systems were discussed in Parts I and II of this book. Here we are concerned primarily with the interactions between nations, and in particular with the factors that lead to the prevalence of war and threats of war in the international marketplace.

In order to maintain its legitimacy, each national government had to provide a sense of security from external threats for its citizens. In order to accomplish this goal, the nation-state had to exert some control over the behavior of other nation-states—at the very least, it had to prevent the armies of other nations from penetrating its own boundaries. Because each nation needed to exert some control over other nations, there was a clear need for some sort of international system that could promote and regulate exchanges among the nations of the world.

THE INTERNATIONAL POLITICAL SYSTEM

The creation of an international political marketplace involved the resolution of an inherent dilemma. On the one hand, the national government could provide security for its citizens only if it maintained complete sovereignty over the national political marketplace. Citizens would give loyal support to the national government only if they perceived it as the authoritative (and just) regulator of exchanges among citizens. On the other hand, the national government could exert influence over the behavior of other nations only by making concessions in return for desired behaviors—in short, by giving up some of its freedom in decision-making. Exchanges between nations, therefore, always involved a conflict between each nation's desire to retain its own complete sovereignty and the necessity of accepting limitations on sovereignty in order to achieve international bargains.

The characteristics of the international marketplace emerge from this conflict. Just as an individual exchanges some freedom of choice in his behavioral alternatives for the benefits of participation in the political marketplace of his society, the nation gives up some autonomy in return for concessions made by other nations. Normally, the nation sacrifices certain resources or options for international activities in order to obtain needed resources and security from attack by other nations. Relatively free from dangers of outside interference, the national government can then turn its attention to the use of available resources to stabilize its internal exchange system. The need for bargaining among nations implied the need for an international marketplace with its own regulations, systems of rewards and sanctions, and—most important—its own political culture including sets of values, beliefs, and expectations.

One of the basic features of the international political culture is the recognition of the dilemma faced by a national government in regard to the maintenance of its sovereignty. Every nation recognizes that a demand for control over the internal marketplace of another nation is a threat to the continued legitimacy of that nation's government. Therefore, such demands are understood to be very extreme and to be appropriate only where the nation making the demand is in a position of overwhelming power. Normally, nations recognize the need to find face-saving solutions to conflicts that will permit each national government to maintain the support of its own citizenry.

The international political system must deal with the wide variety of political cultures that exist in various nations. We have seen that dissatisfied individuals within a nation may identify with alienated subcultures, turning to asystemic or antisystemic activities because they perceive the political system as irrelevant to their own needs and activities. Similarly, a nation will participate in the international system only if it perceives bargaining in that system as relevant to its own needs and perceives the rules and regulations of the marketplace as just according to its own political culture. Because various nations have such different expectations about the kinds of bargains that are just, the evolution of a political system accepted by all nations has been a slow and uncertain process. No international marketplace given complete legitimacy by all nations has ever been developed. Dissatisfied nations have always turned to regional or other international organizations—or to antisystemic actions—when they felt that the prevailing international system was unjust or was failing to meet their demands.

Rapid developments in technology over the past few centuries have posed additional problems for the international political system. When the international system was developed, each nation was concerned primarily with protection against the threat that armies might march over its borders from neighboring nations, or that the navy of another nation might shell its shores. The modern nation must deal with the threats of attack by airplanes or missiles from bases on the other side of the world. Furthermore, modern weaponry carries the possibility of physical destruction far beyond any that could have been conceived a few centuries ago. It has become almost impossible for any nation, even a superpower, to give its citizens a sense of security from external threats.

Advances in communications and transportation have created another source of instability in the world political system. If the typical citizen of a modern nation has not actually visited other nations, he is at least aware of living conditions and events in those nations. The modern national government must convince its citizens that they are receiving a fair share of the world's resources when those citizens have a pretty good idea of the living standard attained by citizens of other nations. It must justify its actions in the international system to citizens who are well informed about those actions and their results. It must attempt to maintain a national political culture and a spirit of national loyalty among citizens who know a great deal about other cultures and about the benefits promised by other nations to their citizens. We have noted the growing tendency for individuals and groups to identify themselves with similar individuals and groups in other nations rather than with the interests of their own national government.

In the face of these developments, it has become increasingly difficult for a modern nation to maintain the spirit of national loyalty that is its major political resource. The need to use external conflicts to inspire patriotism has unfortunately not diminished in the modern world system. It can be argued quite convincingly that a major source of instability in the world today is the frequent resort to war by national governments as a means of overcoming opposition within the nation. Unfortunately, modern weaponry makes this continual warfare a very real threat to the continued survival of our civilization—perhaps to the very survival of life on earth. The need for a stable world political system is more urgent than ever. We turn now to an examination of some elements of the existing world system, focusing particularly upon the factors that encourage the frequent resort to war in international exchanges.

INTERNATIONAL LAW

Within a national marketplace, the national government establishes laws to regulate bargaining exchanges. The citizens recognize the authority of the government to administer sanctions to those who violate the laws. In the international marketplace, there is no legitimate government to enforce international laws. "International law" does exist, but violators of this law are not threatened by a fairly high probability of punishment by a powerful government. Instead, international law is enforced primarily through the fear that a nation stepping outside the limits of the accepted law will suffer high costs because other nations will then feel free to violate the law in their dealings with it. In short, international law can exist only if the great majority of powerful nations feel that observance of the law is beneficial to their interests. These nations will then cooperate in imposing sanctions on any violator of the law.

In a national marketplace, individuals and groups are reinforced for observance of all laws by the fact that the government can provide various benefits for them if it maintains its legitimacy. There is a strong reason for obedience to a law that seems unjust, particularly if there is a perceived opportunity to work within the system to change that law. Because the world marketplace lacks an authoritative government and a well-established system for altering the law peacefully, the individual nation has a strong temptation to violate international law if it seems that such violation will further its immediate interests. The threat of sanctions against lawbreakers is much less direct and much less certain in the international system than in a national system.

The modern body of international law is based fundamentally upon the writings of Hugo Grotius, a seventeenth-century Dutch jurist and statesman. Writing at the time when nation-states were just emerging as the major bargaining agents in the world marketplace, Grotius attempted to set down a systematic body of rules to govern the interactions among nations. Other sources of modern international law are treaties, decisions by the World Court, and custom. Because there is no authoritative government to enforce international law, a law can be effective only if it is generally accepted. Customs that have gradually developed over the centuries are therefore of major importance in international law. These are unwritten, often unstated mores of international behavior that have evolved because they serve the economic and political interests of all states.

For example, the range of a cannon fired from a ship was about three miles. Therefore, it became customary for a nation to treat any ship within three miles of its shoreline as an intruder upon its territory, while other rules evolved to govern interactions of ships beyond the three-mile limit (on the "high seas"). At first, the seafaring nations of Europe observed these patterns of behavior simply because these behaviors were to their mutual benefit. Later, these patterns became customary, and violations of the customs were regarded as violations of international law. The customs were initially reinforced through the willingness of each nation to limit its own behavior in return for the benefits that it received when other nations voluntarily accepted similar limitations. After the customs became accepted as law, a further reinforcement existed because any nation violating the law could expect strong sanctions from other nations besides the one directly affected by the transgression. For example, all (or most) seafaring nations might band together to punish any nation acting in a fashion that the law defined as piracy on the high seas. The sanctions might include refusal of port access to the offending nation, direct attacks upon the ships of that nation, or in the extreme warfare against the home territory of the offending state.

In order to obtain the almost universal support needed to become accepted as international law, a particular custom must be very basic and common to the needs of all nations. The benefits gained by accepting limitations upon freedom of choice must be clearly apparent to every state. If the benefits are less obvious, involving a complex pattern of costs and rewards, the custom is unlikely to become established or to be accepted as a law. Any nation will be likely to violate an international custom or law if it perceives a good chance of obtaining significant benefits by doing so, particularly if that law seems unjust in terms of its national political culture.

Because the nations of western Europe shared many basic beliefs and values in their political cultures, the development of a body of international law governing their interactions was relatively easy— at least in certain areas such as commerce and international travel. Because these nations dominated the oligopolistic world marketplace of the eighteenth and nineteenth centuries, that body of international law was reasonably well respected. (Of course, because compliance with the law was motivated chiefly by a fear of sanctions, the law applied mainly to dealings among the major powers. The violation of law in dealings with weaker nations was usually ignored by other major powers because they desired similar freedom in their dealings with the minor nations.) In the modern world marketplace, the number of nations with significant bargaining power has greatly increased, and the variety of political cultures has become much more extensive. Violations of international law have become much more likely because there are more nations who might see an opportunity to benefit through such violations or who are likely to find accepted laws repugnant or irrelevant to their own political cultures.

There is considerable confusion about the body of law that has practical validity in the modern world marketplace. Is a newly formed nation required to obey a law established through a treaty signed many years ago by the major European powers? Can it be expected to follow a custom that is alien to its own culture? How can a small nation be expected to honor a body of law that the major powers seem to violate with impunity in their dealings with weaker nations? In the absence of a stable international political culture and a long-standing political system, it is not surprising that the newer nations see little benefit in giving their support to a vague body of international law.

Consider the problems of new nations such as those in Africa, whose historical background is very different from that which produced the nation-state in seventeenth-century Europe. The political cultures of these populations are built around systems other than national governments—for example, around the complex ethnolinguistic structures that Europeans termed "tribes." In order to obtain independence from colonial rule, however, these populations had to demand independence as sovereign nations; other potential forms of unity and independence were not recognized in the world marketplace. The political leaders were forced to contrive some form of national political structure in order to gain admittance to the international marketplace and to obtain recognition as bargaining agents for their populations. The African political leaders face the twin problems of imposing a foreign political culture and structure upon their populations and of functioning in an international marketplace whose rules and customs are foreign to their previous experience. Their difficulties are further complicated by the cultural patterns imposed over the past few centuries by the colonial powers in order to further their own interests. It is not surprising that these new governments find great difficulty both in maintaining their legitimacy with their citizenry and in operating effectively in the world marketplace.

One encouraging development in the modern world marketplace is the increasing codification of international law since World War II. Bilateral and multilateral treaties, decisions of the World Court, and resolutions of the United Nations General Assembly have produced a growing body of generally accepted world law that is spelled out in full detail. This development has reduced some of the confusion that surrounded customs and has permitted more precise arrangements to meet the specific needs of modern nations. The trend toward more effective international communication about demands and expectations has been facilitated through the activities of the regional organizations and nongovernmental organizations discussed in Chapter 6.

Yet neither international law nor a more sophisticated international marketplace has succeeded in eliminating violent conflicts among nations. War, violence, subversion, and terror remain all too common characteristics of international exchanges. As we have already suggested, one of the major sources of this instability is the lack of a generally accepted world political culture.

CULTURAL DIFFERENCES AND INTERNATIONAL EXCHANGE

A bargaining agent is likely to accept a compromise—to forego satisfaction of some of his demands—only if he expects that present restraint will lead to future rewards. If he regards the rules and regulations of the marketplace as just, if he feels that scarce resources are distributed fairly in the long run—then he is willing to abide by the rules and to accept the best bargain that he can get at the moment within those rules. If he does not have these perceptions of the rules and the system, he has no incentive to abide by the regulations. In a national marketplace, the government imposes various sanctions to increase the cost of violating its regulations and laws. These sanctions help reduce the likelihood that momentary dissatisfactions will lead to antisystemic actions. In turn, the continued stability of the system reinforces the expectation that law-abiding behavior will produce rewards in the long run.

The lack of such shared expectations and values in the international marketplace makes peaceful bargaining very difficult. If the two agents involved in a bargain have different perceptions about the values of the items being exchanged, they may be unable to agree upon any compromise that seems just to both of them. There is no world government that both parties trust to impose a fair settlement. In the absence of authoritative laws and sanctions, the costs of moving to more violent exchange may seem relatively small in comparison to the possible benefits.

On the other hand, the lack of a shared culture can sometimes be helpful in bargaining. It may happen that one nation is seeking something that is of little value to the other nation, while the second nation can obtain in exchange something of great value to it and of little value to the first nation. Unfortunately, this simple paradigm seldom applies to actual international bargaining.

There are certain basic desires that seem to be shared by all nation-states: increased power in the world marketplace, the ability to influence the behavior of other nations, and the ability to make decisions with maximum freedom from interference by other nations. Many factors are involved in determining the power of a nation, including natural resources, technological capacity, geography, military prowess, sophistication of the economic system, and cohesiveness of the political society. Clearly, nations differ in the power that they can exert in the world marketplace. When nations seek new markets or new spheres of influence, these scarce resources become the objects of international competition as each nation seeks to invest some of its present power in order to obtain increased future power. Because every nation places a very high value upon the resources that contribute to its power, it will be willing to pay a very high price in order to secure these resources. When the two competing parties are fairly evenly matched in military power and when the risk of external sanctions seems low, the option of risking all on the possibility of victory in a war may seem quite attractive to both parties.

Because of the intensity of demands for scarce resources, diplomatic negotiations often become stalemated when neither side is willing preted by another. In a conflict between two nations, one nation might take an action that it regards as a face-saving but inherently conciliatory gesture. The second nation—interpreting the action in its own cultural terms—may regard the gesture as a belligerent or insulting one. Even if the political leaders of the second nation interpret the action correctly, they must deal with the fact that modern communications will give their citizenry a full account of the events, and that the citizenry may be less able to understand the culture of the other nation. Thus, the leaders may feel obliged to respond to the act in a way that will retain the support of the citizens for the government, even if the response is an inappropriate one that increases the likelihood of war. The high stakes, scarce resources, and continual possibility of misinterpretation in today's loosely structured forum for international exchange make the process of international bargaining highly volatile and unstable.

DIPLOMACY

Diplomacy is a tactic that emerged early in the game of international politics as a way to increase the effectiveness of bargaining. A nation seeks to advance its interests in the world marketplace through diplomacy—either through secret negotiations with other countries or in open discussions that exert pressure upon other nations to act or refrain from acting in certain ways. In the 1970s, the United States secretary of state, Henry Kissinger, has engaged in both secret and open diplomacy in his efforts to defuse potential regional conflicts while simultaneously advancing the interests of the United States. For example, Kissinger has used public threats and statements of position as well as secret negotiations in an effort to achieve a peaceful settlement of the conflict between Israel and its Arab neighbors. Kissinger has sought not only to avoid a war that could disrupt the world political system, but also to increase the power and influence of the United States in the Middle East.

Unfortunately, the settlement of a dispute does not always coincide with the advancement of the interests of a powerful nation. For example, it seems probable that United States actions in Southeast Asia prolonged regional conflicts that would have been settled much sooner in the absence of outside interference. In this case, the United States acted because it feared that the settlements reached would be harmful to its interests.

The art of diplomacy is a delicate one. When nations are competing for scarce resources, they are likely to make very strong demands and to view compromises as unacceptable. The diplomat must try to understand the values and needs of each nation and to find just the right balance of benefits and costs that will produce a bargain acceptable to all nations involved. He must contend with the fact that national leaders may be using the dispute as a way of enhancing their legitimacy, and that the leaders of a nation will not accept a bargain if they perceive a danger of losing domestic support when their citizenry learns about the bargain. The diplomat must sense and overcome misperceptions that airse from differing cultural viewpoints.

Because of the intensity of demands for scarce resources, diplomatic negotiations often become stalemated when neither side is willing to offer as much as the other side demands. In such cases, progress is usually possible only if threats of sanctions (such as military action) are added to the bargain to increase the costs of the dispute and make compromise seem more desirable to all parties concerned. However, if no acceptable settlement is reached, a nation may then feel obliged to carry through on its threats of military action in order to preserve its credibility in future negotiations.

At its best, diplomacy is one technique for facilitating bargaining between nations and seeking peaceful exchanges in the international marketplace. It is not a substitute for international law or organization. It has proved particularly useful in settling disputes between major powers and in resolving conflicts between minor powers in cases where the major powers find it in their interests to prevent a regional war. However, if a major power perceives a regional conflict as beneficial to its own interests, that power may well act to impede settlement of the conflict or even to exert its own political and military power on behalf of one party to the conflict. In such cases where diplomacy proves useless, international organizations sometimes can play a role in preventing or limiting violence.

INTERNATIONAL ORGANIZATION

Regional organizations, whose members have a shared interest in avoiding the costs of local wars, usually provide the first level of organized efforts to prevent or halt outbreaks of violence between nations. The members of the regional organization may be able to facilitate a peaceful settlement between the warring nations, drawing upon the shared cultures and interests of the region. In some cases, threats of sanctions imposed by the organization or its other members may be sufficient to halt the conflict.

If regional organizations fail to halt a conflict, the United Nations provides an international forum where the dispute can be debated openly and where other nations can exert political influence to seek a settlement. In some cases, compliance with a resolution of the General Assembly can provide a face-saving alternative to further violence for both sides of the dispute.

In practice, however, the United Nations has proved relatively impotent in settling disputes that involve the interests of the major powers. It was unable, for example, to take any significant action to halt the conflict in Vietnam. Furthermore, all efforts to halt a conflict— through diplomacy, international organizations, or the intervention of major powers—are likely to fail if the nations involved place extremely high values upon the issues of the dispute. In the war over the secession of Biafra from Nigeria, for example, both sides felt that a complete victory was essential to their survival. The leaders of Biafra believed that any settlement failing to give them independence would result in the elimination of their culture and even their population by the Nigerian government. The leaders of Nigeria believed that the survival of the Nigerian nation depended upon retention of Biafra as part of the nation. If a nation believes that its continued existence depends upon satisfaction of its demands, it is hardly likely to accept a compromise. The impasse will not be resolved through sanctions imposed by major powers or international organizations because no cost attached to continued struggle could outweigh the perceived cost of surrender.

TRANSNATIONAL GROUPS

We have already noted the appearance of transnational groups that represent coalitions of individuals who perceive shared interests and goals. Members of such groups seek to exert influence in the international marketplace outside the channels provided by national governments, as well as seeking to use combined resources within each national marketplace. The oil industry, for example, operates as an organized transnational unit that formulates policies, seeks to influence all national governments to adopt those policies, and even acts through OPEC as an agent in the international marketplace. One might applaud this kind of development as a realistic realignment of the political structure suitable to the "global village" created by modern communications and transportation. In the modern world, the nation-state seems unable to provide cultural or physical security for its citizens; perhaps transnational organizations represent the first step toward the creation of a new and more efficient political system on a world scale. Even if this is true, however, the existence of transnational organizations creates very serious problems and instabilities in the existing political system.

Whatever its failures, the nation-state at least established a very basic set of shared values and expectations in the international marketplace. Even if no complete international political culture could be established, nations could interact with reasonable expectations about the results of their behavior. There was hope that even greater stability could be achieved in the international market if standards were spelled out more clearly and if the benefits and costs of various actions could be predicted more accurately. Nations could postpone satisfaction of some demands in the belief that maintenance of some world order would eventually bring benefits to justify their restraint. Certain forms of behavior were voluntarily avoided because the costs of violating international custom were perceived as too high.

The appearance of transnational groups seems to be disrupting even this minimal order that had been achieved among nation-states. These groups have no accepted place in the international market; because they are not nation-states, they are not recognized as bargaining agents for their members. Therefore, these groups are likely to place a high value upon a radical restructuring of the international political system. They reject the accepted rules and customs of the marketplace and thus introduce an element of unpredictability and chaos into the system.

Groups using international terrorist activities—for example, the Black September fringe of the Palestinean movement—represent an extreme case of this new factor in the international system. The terrorist group regards the rules of both national and international marketplaces as irrelevant to its demands and goals. It defies sanctions threatened by national governments and even is willing to accept the opposition of powerful political sectors in various nations. The terrorist group seeks its support from dissident factions in many different nations. It uses modern systems of international communications and transportation as important tools in its effort to disrupt existing political systems, attract support from antisystemic forces, and obtain resources to support its activities. To some extent, members of such a group may simply derive satisfaction and psychological benefit through the sense of power and attention that they receive. More importantly, however, these groups view themselves as alienated from the existing political systems. They accept the high costs of their activities because they perceive no rewards to be obtained through cooperation with the system. Feeling that they have no chance of obtaining meaningful benefits within the system, they are willing to accept the risk of destroying the system and hoping to fare better under the resulting anarchy or under any new system that is created. Furthermore, the failure of the system to halt the activities of the terrorists becomes a reward in itself, because terrorist threats then become commodities that can be offered in exchange for desired concessions by political leaders.

Other transnational organizations use techniques less extreme than those of the terrorist groups. Nonetheless, their operation outside the rules of the system does create uncertainty about expectations and therefore creates instability in the system. Until a new political system develops in which these organizations can play a well-defined role and can obtain benefits through activities that support the system, the transnational organizations will remain as disturbing and destabilizing influences in the international marketplace.

SUMMARY

The current international political marketplace is a complex and rapidly evolving system. The rules and structures are in a state of flux. Compared to most national political marketplaces, the international marketplace is poorly defined and its groundrules are vague.

A recent ruling of the World Court illustrates both the strengths and the weakenesses of the amorphous structures and vague guidelines of the international political system. Under a mandate of the League of Nations in 1919, the Union of South Africa was given full powers of legislation and administration over the territory of Southwest Africa. After World War II, pressure arose to force South Africa to turn the territory over to United Nations administration. South Africa claimed the right to continue its rule over the territory, arguing that nothing in international law required it to turn its mandate over to the UN. In 1950, the World Court issued an advisory opinion confirming South Africa's position, but requiring South Africa to submit reports to the UN about its administration of the territory. During following years, the World Court twice more upheld South Africa's right to continue its mandate over Southwest Africa.

In 1960, Ethiopia and Liberia filed a complaint with the World Court, charging that South Africa had failed to fulfill its obligations under the terms of the original League of Nations mandate. In 1962 the Court agreed to consider the case, and the South African government filed a defense of its actions with the Court. In 1966, the Court finally handed down a decision holding that Ethiopia and Liberia lacked any legal interest in the matter and therefore were not qualified to make any complaint. The Third World factions that had been seeking UN supervision and eventual independence for Southwest Africa were dismayed by the Court's failure to consider the central legal issue. They took the matter to the UN General Assembly, which had already shown sympathy for the Third World position by earlier blocking South African efforts to incorporate the territory into the South African nation. Within a few months, the General Assembly voted to end South Africa's mandate over the territory.

In 1968, the General Assembly created a special council of 11 nations to take over administration of the territory and lead it to independence, giving it the name of Namibia. South Africa continued to insist upon its legal right to rule the territory, and the South African government refused to admit UN representatives into the area. In 1970, the Security Council passed a resolution condemning South Africa for "illegal" control of Namibia, and the next year the World Court issued an opinion agreeing that South Africa's rule was illegal. Although various nations have imposed trading sanctions against South Africa because of its actions, these sanctions have not been very effective, and the territory remains under South African rule.

On the one hand, the international political system has functioned in this case to provide various forums for debate and bargaining about the dispute; the debates have apparently satisfied all parties sufficiently to prevent an outbreak of war. On the other hand, the system has certainly not functioned efficiently or swiftly, and the outcomes of the various proceedings have had very little effect upon the realities of the situation. Both the United Nations and the World Court have proved largely impotent to enforce their decisions because the major nations have not chosen to put strong pressure on South Africa to obey those decisions. It can be argued that the World Court acted very weakly, refusing to issue a substantive opinion on the dispute until after a firm position had been taken by the United Nations.

Institutions and structures do exist for regulation of bargaining among nations. Despite cultural differences and diverse expectations among nations engaged in international political exchange, certain minimal rules are followed and certain basic values are shared. In the case of Southwest Africa, all parties to the dispute have at least been willing to postpone violent conflict while seeking to resolve the matter through the structures of the international system. Lacking cohesive guidelines and a government able to make authoritative decisions and impose sanctions, however, the international marketplace remains diffuse and unstable. Resort to violence and warfare is not uncommon in international exchange.

. The promise of more orderly forms for effecting change and resolving disputes is still offered by international organizations of all kinds, and acceptance of their rules and authority seems to be growing. Nations seem to share an increasing awareness of mutual interdependence despite great differences and of the high cost of instability and violence in the modern world. On the other hand, rapid changes in the nature of the marketplace are leading to new kinds of instability. If the international political system is to become fully effective and stable, it must instill confidence in all who seek results from its processes—confidence that rewards will be distributed in an acceptable manner. Furthermore, it must provide access and responses to the demands of groups and organizations that are developing across national borders.

REFERENCES

Brierly, James. L. *The Law of Nations.* Oxford: Clarendon Press, 1963.
Herz, John H. *International Politics in the Atomic Age.* New York: Columbia Univ. Press, 1959.
Morgenthau, Hans J. *Politics Among Nations.* New York: Knopf, 1967.

Conclusion

Let us now summarize our discussion and reexamine the exchange model, highlighting its advantages and possible shortcomings as a framework for political analysis.

From the beginning of this book, we have assumed that choice (individual and collective) is basic to politics, political processes, and political institutions. We do not mean to imply that each person is always aware of his choices or of the consequences of every alternative choice. We are simply assuming that it is useful to conceptualize politics in terms of choices. To amplify this statement somewhat, we find it useful to consider the array of choices available to individuals and groups at a given time, the consequences of those choices, and the balance accepted between advantages gained and those given up in the actual choices that are made. This approach to the analysis of politics has led us to the model of political exchange. The act of choosing entails making an exchange because one alternative is given up or exchanged for another in the process of choosing.

We thus have described and analyzed politics in terms of possible choices and the exchanges inherent in those choices. The logic of exchange analysis rests on the assumption that the behavior of an individual can be explained by his effort to maximize the satisfaction that he will obtain from the results of his actions. We accept the proposition that this maximization of satisfaction underlies the process of choice and exchange.

Using exchange analysis, we have attempted to produce an understandable and logical view of politics—from individual political behavior, through the political dynamics of various political groups and sectors and institutions, to the behavior of nation states. We believe that exchange analysis has enabled us to deal with these various levels of analysis without falling into traps that often ensnare the political analyst who seeks to transfer approaches and concepts from one level of analysis to another. Political acts of individuals and groups, in whatever form they appear, can be described as choices among alternatives; in turn, the interactions of choice-making individuals or groups and the acts of choosing among alternatives can be described as exchanges. We believe that this brief text shows that the exchange model can provide a useful description of political behavior at all levels of interaction, from that of individuals to that of nations.

In its emphasis on choice and exchange, the exchange model borrows from economic theory a long-standing preference for analysis in terms of individual decisions. That is, our viewpoint interprets the acts and decisions of groups, organizations, and nations both (1) as the product of individual acts and decisions and (2) as analogous to individual acts and decisions. The value of this approach must be measured by the extent to which its use elucidates various political concepts (such as legitimacy and modernization), describes various political institutions (such as legislatures and parties), and explains the behavior of various political actors (such as nations and international organizations). In using this approach, the political analyst must of course recognize that the variables and the environment change drastically as he moves from one level of analysis to another, even though the basic principles of the model are retained.

Of necessity, we have presented a somewhat simplified view of politics in this book. This simplification is not the result of any shortcoming of the exchange model but rather of an intentionally limited use of the model to provide a brief and clear introduction to political science. Political analysts have indeed applied the exchange model to politics with great rigor, as can be seen in many of the works cited in this text. Our objective here has not been to illustrate the exactitude or rigor of the exchange model but simply to provide an introduction to political analysis that emphasizes the unity underlying the apparent diversity of the political universe.

We turn now from this consideration of our approach to a review of the basic argument of this text. In Part I, we attempted to accomplish two major goals. First, we introduced the reader to the concepts of exchange and to the nature and scope of politics itself. Second, we used the exchange model to explore certain areas of interest to political scientists, including political culture, legitimacy, social and political change, and revolution. The areas we chose to discuss in the limited space available were selected because they allowed us to introduce key concepts used in other parts of the book. Emphasis on these areas helped to show the unity of political analysis at all levels, and enabled us to demonstrate the utility of these concepts as we turned to comparative politics in Part II.

Part II turned from the treatment of politics in the abstract to the discussion of national political systems. The discussion centered on the political institutions and political processes found in the United States, using this familiar political system as the major example of a national system. We then provided a comparative perspective by discussing two major types of national exchange systems. Competitive industrial systems similar to that of the United States were compared and contrasted in a general discussion of the evolution of political culture in France, Great Britain, and Germany. Noncompetitive idustrial systems, such as the U.S.S.R., were then contrasted with the preceding type by an emphasis on the relative roles played by coercion and information in the two types of system. Further perspective was provided by a discussion of the nonindustrialized world and of modernization in China.

In planning Part II, we chose this approach as the best way to give the reader insight into specific institutions and processes, while allowing him to generalize beyond the United States to legislatures and processes of rule-making in other systems. The discussion of competitive and noncompetitive systems was designed to provide an overview of the context in which institutions function. The discussion of modernization and the Third World emphasized forces and problems that are of rapidly growing importance. The topics of Part II were chosen to alert the reader to the problems and rewards of cross-national analysis, without slighting the complexities and nuances that characterize both American and comparative politics.

Turning in Part III to international politics and organizations, we used exchange analysis not only to describe but to unite what at times seems a very confusing and esoteric field of study. We discussed types of international systems, alliances, détente, and international, regional, and nongovernmental organizations, concluding with a discussion of war and terrorism. Again, available space limited our choice of topics, but we sought an adequate combination of historically persistent concerns and current issues that promise to remain of importance in coming years.

Throughout this text, we have tried to discuss specific examples of political interaction, both to illustrate the exchange analysis and to demonstrate the versatility of our approach in describing and analyzing the specifics of diverse policies. Such analysis of particular political events helps make more meaningful our discussion of, say, the presidency or of local government. Such specific applications of the exchange model also are of great importance in showing the value of the model, because they enable us to analyze public policy as the end product of exchanges and choices. Any policy represents the making of specific choices for a society. We feel that the approach used here is well suited to the examination of general political concepts, and that it strikes an appropriate balance between the general and the specific—an important consideration for an introductory text. The inclusion of specific examples increases the probability that the reader will achieve a firmer understanding of the generalizations, and helps him to test his understanding against the details of real events. Specific examples also lead to questions about the relationships between (1) institutions and processes and (2) public policies. This brief introductory text cannot adequately answer all the questions that may be triggered by the discussion of specific examples, but we trust that it does give the reader a frame of reference that will help him to draw his own conclusions and make further generalizations.

Political science is a discipline that has been characterized by a number of contending approaches and hypotheses. Without ignoring the potential problems of exchange analysis, we believe that it offers a flexibility that makes it a useful basic approach to the field and that enables its blending with other approaches to teaching and research. It is in this realm of dynamic analysis that political science often falls short of its goals. Exchange analysis shows a marked ability to offer insights into the dynamic relationships between variables, unlike other approaches that emphasize categorization or static models. Further attention must be given to increasing the rigor and quantitative application of the exchange model in political analysis. We believe that existing studies have demonstrated the possibility of such refinement of the approach.

In this concluding section, we have attempted to provide an overview of the text and, more importantly, to highlight some of the advantages and problems attendant upon the use of exchange analysis. We hope that the reader will come away with a clearer appreciation of the complexity of political processes, and with an enhanced ability to analyze the political interactions of individuals and groups.

Index